IF I WERE THE BOSS OF YOU

"This writer's authentic voice reminds me of all the Southern women I have known and loved."

—**Winston Groom, author of *Forrest Gump***

"Melinda Rainey Thompson writes with dazzling wit, thoughtful insight, and a deep wisdom that we need more than ever these days. You don't want to miss this jewel of a book!"

—**Cassandra King Conroy, bestselling author of**
***The Sunday Wife, The Same Sweet Girls,* and**
Tell Me a Story

"[This is] a beautiful baby of a book that is destined to keep you up all night . . . . Debra and I stayed up the first night reading and laughing out loud and reading and laughing and reading. And the next night. And the next . . . . this is the best stuff we've read of its kind since we first fell in love with the writings of Fannie Flagg, Rheta Grimsley Johnson, and a host of other favorites. The wit is refreshing and needed, especially in these politically charged times when everyone's favorite pastime is spewing their spirited opinions upon the masses."

—**Charles Ghigna, poet and author**

"Melinda Rainey Thompson has an uncanny way of telling stories about seemingly ordinary events to remind us all of our shared humanity. Humorous, authentic, thought-provoking, and delightful."

—Westina Matthews, author of *Dancing from the Inside Out: Grace-Filled Reflections on Growing Older*

"Melinda Thompson's new book *If I Were The Boss of You* presents a problem: How do you describe it? Philosophy? Plato, Socrates and Aristotle could learn life lessons from Melinda; Manners? Following this book's advice will make the reader appear to be a Southern lady regardless of her beginnings; Humor? Probably the best choice—but only if you're really, really extra smart."

—Jake Reiss, The Alabama Booksmith

"I think we're ready for a book that delves into the mysteries of the Southern Woman of the 21st Century, but I'm not sure we're all ready for Melinda Rainey Thompson. She is standing a little too close for comfort, telling the truth in a way that is challenging without being confrontational, vulnerable without asking for sympathy. This is a fun book, but not 'light reading.' Like every sermon I've ever tried to preach, this book made me laugh, and cry, and think."

—The Rt. Rev. Kee Sloan, Bishop of the Episcopal Diocese of Alabama

"Don't let Melinda Thompson's reputation as a humorist fool you. *If I Were The Boss of You* is funny, very funny but if you're not careful she'll smack you in the face. Sometimes a piece of humor can make you laugh and squirm at the same time. Thompson captures the insanity (and hilarity) of daily extant causing you to face mortality, smelly babies, piracy, leaky memories, anticipation, and even dread. I faced it all and came out the other side a happier man."

—Lee Hurley, Publisher, WHY Media

If I Were the Boss of You:
A Southern Woman's
Guide to the Sweet Life

by Melinda Rainey Thompson

ISBN 978-1-63393-997-4

Published by

◤ köehlerbooks™

210 60th Street
Virginia Beach, VA 23451
800–435–4811
www.koehlerbooks.com

IF I WERE THE BOSS OF YOU

A Southern Woman's Guide to the Sweet Life

MELINDA RAINEY THOMPSON

VIRGINIA BEACH
CAPE CHARLES

CONTENTS

Section VII: In My Opinion

Section VIII: The Real World

Section IX: Head Toward The Light

Section X: My Life's Work

Section XI: Past and Present

Dear Reader,

Originally, this book had a much more dignified working title. In the end, I decided to go with *If I Were the Boss of You*. I'm fond of this title. It feels right to me. How many times did you yell, "You aren't the boss of me!" to your sister or brother when you were growing up? And if you are wondering about whether it should be *If I Was the Boss of You* instead, read about the conditional tense. I love English grammar. I really do.

All three of my offspring have said to me, at one point or another, "What do you know?" in that snotty, condescending voice teenagers mysteriously acquire at the onset of puberty. I stand by the response that flew out of my mouth the first time those words were hurled in my direction: "I know *plenty!*"

While I was writing this book, I became obsessed with recurring themes, questions, regrets, and longings. I am intrigued by the concepts of memory, choices, perspective, point of view, and what happens after we exit the earthly stage for the last time—after a long, illustrious life filled with standing ovations and sixteen curtain calls or, unexpectedly, through a hidden trapdoor in the floor or via a hook dragging us off the stage screaming, cursing, and holding on to the curtain with both hands.

As usual, I discovered that I am not alone in my thoughts. Many of you are concerned about the same issues that worry me. This isn't surprising since there is nothing special about me. If I inspired an action figure, she would be called Ordinary Woman, and she would look nothing like Barbie. The only real difference between you and me is that I do my musing on paper in front of God and everybody. It's high-risk work. My family often wishes I would pursue another profession.

I've learned some life lessons that I'm willing to share. I feel very civic-minded about it, actually, like I've braved a thunderstorm to vote in a primary election or dragged my recycling to the curb. You shouldn't heed my advice just because I'm getting older, however. We are all aging. It's not just me, thank God. Old age does not necessarily convey wisdom. Every old piece of furniture isn't a prize antique. Some of it's junk. The beauty of this book is: you get to decide what to keep and what to throw out.

I'm bossy enough to think I know what's best for almost everyone. Just ask my children. They'll tell you. Maybe you can help me by spreading the word. Get to work on those online book reviews—as long as you love the book, of course. Otherwise, I think it's best if you keep your opinions to yourself.

I hope you learn from my mistakes. That's the point here. More than anything, I hope you laugh out loud when you read some of these chapters and put your head down on your arms and cry when you read others. I hope you lie awake at night thinking about the content of this book, and I hope you find your own life in these pages. My most fervent desire is that you will read one sentence in this book that you remember forever because it rings true to you all the way down to your bones.

Fondly,

Mel

LEST WE FORGET

———————✤———————

WHILE WRITING THIS BOOK, I seem to have accidentally begun exploring the concept of memory. I assure you I didn't plan to do this. My initial *Table of Contents* for this book was unrecognizable by the time I finished it, an eventuality which actually caused me to bang my head against the wall and eat an entire party-sized bag of peanut M&Ms. Writer frustration, carbohydrates, sugar, and liquor go hand in hand. I'm not the first writer to go down that road. Fitzgerald. Hemingway. Faulkner. Just to name a few. Good company when you think about it. I've even got the crazy family, too. Peanut M&M binging is the *best-case* scenario in those biographies. You'll see. The truth is that I often sit down to write an essay about one subject and end up writing about something entirely different.

I'm not fond of this turn of events. It throws me off my game because I'm a planner by nature. I don't like it when my brain calls an audible. Also, I'm not a neurosurgeon, so I can't make adjustments to my brain or anyone else's like I adjust the settings on my iPhone. That would be handy, I think. Addiction problem? Get a little tune-up. Depression? Head to a spa for a tweak. Science may really take us there in the not-too-distant future. I hope so. Meanwhile, I secretly fear that my brain processes information differently than other people's brains, that I'm not only ha-ha funny but also funny-peculiar. I don't think I want to delve too deeply into my own crazy. Do you? Who knows what is really going on in there? Like the rest of my quirks, I've become comfortable in my own skin, and I've chosen to find myself charming.

Sometimes, I get inspired writing material when I let my mind wander, so who am I to question good results? Does this happen to you, too? Do you have mental digressions when you are going about your regular, grocery-shopping, errand-running day? Do you find yourself turning over problems in your mind when you take out the garbage, walk your dog, or stand in line for deli meat?

I think weighty topics bubble to the surface of our brains when we aren't consciously thinking about anything at all, and our brains are on autopilot. When our brains are only occupied with keeping us breathing, avoiding painful stimuli—generally keeping us alive and safe from harm—that's when our brain cells say to one another, "Hey, since we have a little free time, and there's nothing big going on at work today, how about we figure out how to split up the Middle East and keep everybody happy? And while we're at it, maybe we could get everyone to join hands, sing 'We Are The World,' clean up the environment, and spread some food around so everybody goes to bed with a full belly tonight. That would be good." I admit the process is a bit more scientific than that, but I think you know what I mean.

I can't lay off the subject of memory. Maybe it's my age. Turning fifty really put a twist in my knickers. For the last couple of years, whenever I misplace the kitchen scissors or buy mustard three times in a row at the store because I can't remember if I've already bought it or not, I worry that I have Alzheimer's disease. I think about potential "brain food" now when I stand in the grocery store aisle reading labels, and I'm considering taking up crossword puzzles as a hobby, even though I don't enjoy working them. I've recently given up diet sodas because of the potential link to Alzheimer's, and I fear it might be easier to kick a heroin habit. I'm struggling with that little addiction because I need my brain cells firing on all cylinders until the day I die. Reading and writing, public speaking, and teaching others to read and write is how I make my living. If I can't do those things at a high-functioning level, I'm toast.

The science behind memory makes for fascinating nightstand reading if you're interested in the research like I am. Our individual memories are what make us unique—not just *human*, but one specific human. Our collective memory defines us as a people. No matter how imperfect, selective, subjective, and faulty our memories are, they are precious to us. A disease that wipes one's memory clean—like a hard drive being stripped of its identifying markers before being tossed into a trash heap—is a cruel fate for anyone but particularly those whose life's work depends on all those neurons being able to connect. Brain MRIs that show white clumps of plaque indicate portions of the brain that are dead and never coming back. I'm not sure we were ever meant to see such things.

I understand why prisoners scratch hash marks into their cell walls to mark the passage of time. It helps them remember each day individually in an environment where the days run together in a monotonous stream. We humans want to remember and be remembered. This desire is innate, I believe. A hash mark on the wall, street graffiti, a shout-out into the abyss of social media—all those pleas say the same thing: "I was here! Notice me! Remember me!"

At some point, we all feel the passage of time differently. It seems to speed up or slow down, depending on our feelings of anticipation, excitement, fear, or dread—the countdown to a wedding, milestone birthday, or holiday, the birth of a baby, the results of a medical test, a verdict from a jury, or waiting for a soldier to return from war, for example. We've all experienced this. Time is inflexibly analog. It marches relentlessly in a straight line. I always envision it as one of those illustrated timelines that teachers taped above blackboards in classrooms when I was in school. The Evolution of Humankind. The Industrial Revolution. The Spread of the Roman Empire. Civil Rights in America. Each hash mark and incremental dot represents real-life blood spilled, families torn asunder, and dreams fulfilled or crushed in infancy by mere happenstance of geography, skin color, birth order, gender, or political whim.

We need our memories. Happy memories sustain us, remind us who we are, what we hold dear, and whom we love. They are a testament to what we've done with the time allotted to us on earth. It's not just happy memories that define us, of course. Unhappy memories change us for good or ill, too. After all, what parent who has lost a child would trade the happy memories of that child's birth and life, however brief, in order to avoid the grief? Even our marriages and friendships, those that didn't last a lifetime as we'd initially hoped, contained transcendent moments of happiness, laughter, and joy. We are a product of all that we are born with and all that we experience in our lives—the good, the bad, the ugly, and the indifferent.

That's not such a terrible truth.

THE MEMORY VAULT

———————❧———————

I THINK THE DISTANCE between those of us who are alive and well here on earth and our daisy-pushing friends and relatives isn't very far at all. This has become a recurring theme in my writing. I prefer to think of this predilection as a charming eccentricity rather than a freaky obsession, but I admit it's a little Stephen King-ish. The distance can seem paper thin sometimes, as if you could whisk it aside like a curtain made of gossamer linen and touch someone on the other side. Wherever that is. Or is it *when*ever? Consciousness, eternal life, something after this life on earth . . . it's a tricky business.

I'm not the only person I know who reports occasionally feeling the presence of a long-gone-but-still-longed-for someone close to me. I'm just the only person I know who will admit it without the excuse of being tipsy to justify the imaginative dive in the light of day. You can read a million stories about this kind of thing on the Internet, so it must be a real phenomenon, regardless of whether or not it's actually true, right? Yeti, Bigfoot, dragons, Elvis, the Loch Ness Monster—all those sightings of legend and lore begin with some kernel of truth, mistaken identify, or superstition, I suspect. Ghosts, specters, angels, immortal souls, call them what you will; it's the cast of thousands from campy horror movies. Here's the deal: stereotypes, generalizations, urban myths . . . they all start somewhere to attempt to explain, justify, reinvent, inspire, preserve, circumvent, imagine, codify, prejudice, indoctrinate, or mythologize some event, person, way of life, or viewpoint for other humans. This is how we connect with one another in every culture, every time period, everywhere on earth since we dipped our hands in mud and blood and slapped them on cave walls to call out to the universe: I. Was. Here.

I once walked into a room and was sure my recently deceased grandmother had just turned the corner into the hall. I hadn't even been thinking about her before the incident. I would have sworn on a stack of Bibles that I caught a glimpse of her skirt out of the corner of my eye, and I could sense movement in the air. I even thought I smelled a hint of her face powder. Really. I'm not crazy, and I'm not making this up. Why would I?

Maybe these moments are mental manifestations of grief. The brain is capable of some impressive sleight of hand, but it felt real to me at the time. I don't have the degrees to pursue this line of research, but I sure find it interesting. Scientists have only scratched the surface of what our brains are capable of doing for us. An elaborate hoax perpetrated by our brains to keep a memory safe in our long-term storage, easily accessible, and handy as a source of comfort seems like it would be easy work for the thousands of neurons firing away in our noggins.

Nothing is black and white or decidedly one thing or another anymore. This includes life and death. In one part of a hospital, everything imaginable can be working to keep an unborn baby or a terminally ill person alive. In another part of the same hospital on the same day, an unborn child of the same gestational age can be aborted, or a terminally ill person may have chosen to abandon further treatment. The world is complicated. It has always been complicated. We are just becoming more aware, and medicine and technology have taken us to places with ramifications we could not have imagined twenty years ago.

My daughter complained recently about her homework. "There's a lot more to learn than when you were in school, Mom!" she said.

"You're right," I confirmed, "and the information is compounding at some exponential rate that I can't figure out because I can't do the math. You better get on that," I urged.

Every year I live I find myself dwelling more and more on the gray areas of life. When I was young, I had the zeal of a freedom fighter—right was right, and wrong was wrong. Now I see how naïve, narrow, and unkind that view often is.

There was a time when gender identity was considered a clear either/or assignment. Now we know there's a lot of room for flexibility on that topic. History confirms that these struggles aren't new. What's new is our mainstream awakening to them.

Fighting between nation-states and smaller factions, groups, and individuals presents similarly murky questions. Is any one life worth more than another? How about animal rights?

The line between life and death is blurry now. There is no on/off switch to signal the beginning of life or the end of it. It's more of a sliding scale: asleep, unconscious, comatose, persistent vegetative state, brain dead . . . dead. The more we learn about the brain, the more colors we can see on the color wheel.

I've become quite a fan of the brain. I corner every neurologist I meet socially and pepper him or her with questions. (Avoid diet sodas, I've learned from my informal interrogations of chatty neurologists. They may lead to dementia.)

I have a friend in Mississippi who says she felt the presence of her mother, a woman long dead, when she was canning fresh pears, a useful skill her mother taught her. In her head, she heard each instruction in her mother's voice, and she found herself going through each step carefully, just as she'd been taught so many years ago. A chore turned into a blessing as almost-forgotten memories washed over her in waves.

Our memories comfort us sometimes and torture us upon occasion, too, in a never-ending loop of pleasure, regret, grief, longing, nostalgia, anger, resentment, and love. Happy or sad, these recorded bits and pieces, archived carefully in our long-term memory banks, define us, both as individuals, members of our respective tribes, and as tiny specks on the collective timeline of Homo sapiens.

ANGELS AND ALIENS

DO YOU BELIEVE IN ghosts? How about angels or aliens? Every time one of my children asks me whether or not I believe in something like that, I always hedge my bets, waffle around, and avoid any definitive answer. That's because I don't know what to say or how to answer the question. I'm an artful dodger. Teachers and moms are good at that, and I'm both of those.

"Yes," "no," "maybe," "upon occasion," and "a little bit" aren't very satisfying answers. We humans prefer neat categories of right and wrong, real or fake, and good or bad. Sadly, almost nothing is that simple. I am a practical, neat, organized, and logical type of person. I don't like vagueness any more than you do, believe me, and online conspiracy nuts make me reach for the Advil.

What I know to be true is that throughout our recorded history on this planet, when we humans have been certain that we know everything there is to know about something (which we've done over and over), that "fact"—or "alternative fact"—always turns out to be wrong or, at the very least, incomplete. When you think about it, humans are remarkably arrogant, considering how easily the species could be wiped out. One good year for viruses, and we're goners. Knock out the bee population, for example, and we may very well go extinct. We need those pesky insects for pollination—to feed ourselves. One epic global pandemic, and it's back to the dark ages for us humans. Our immune systems are rather delicate. I'm afraid that is what will get us in the end.

"The world is flat!" our ancestors said, positively. "Be careful, or you'll sail over the edge!"

Well, no, as it turns out, you won't.

"Humans can't walk on the moon! That's Hollywood trickery," plenty of people scoffed. True, it took us a while to figure out how to get Neil Armstrong off the ship and on the moon for a stroll while also ensuring we could bring him back alive, but we eventually found a way. That should be the motto for us mortals: Humans Will Find a Way. Arrogant but also endearing—that's us.

"If humans were meant to fly, we'd have wings!" the masses shouted. The Wright brothers were discounted over and over and lived through failure after failure. Almost no one believed they could really pull it off. They didn't have grant money, venture capital, crowdsourcing, or anything but their own wits and brawn to fall back on, but they believed in themselves. They had faith. They dared to dream big. So did others who made a difference in the world: Jonas Salk, Dietrich Bonhoeffer, Bill Gates, Rosa Parks, and Albert Einstein. "I think I can! I think I can!" shouted the little engine in *The Little Engine That Could.*

Most theologies are based on a belief in something believers can never prove to the satisfaction of non-believers. That is the essence of faith. It would be a further example of our arrogance, I believe, to think that we know all there is to know about this world, the ones that came before, or the ones that might come after. We all began as stardust, quite literally. I find that a little romantic. Do you?

I think the strongest force on earth is love. Not fear. Not desire. Not hatred. Love. I know it exists. I've experienced it personally and observed it in others, but I can't quantify it precisely, demonstrate it in a laboratory, or prove empirically that love is the end-all and be-all for humans, although I believe it from somewhere so deep within me that no one could ever convince me otherwise.

Have you ever noticed that a dying person's last words—no matter how spiteful, vicious, trying, arrogant, or hateful that person has been in his or her life—are almost always words of love? Rarely do you hear of someone going into the great goodnight while railing and cursing. And I don't think that's because we get more polite when we're dying. I think we just get more honest. Dying is the ultimate stripping bare, for each of us, to what really matters. We all come into the world and leave it with nothing but what's contained within our own skins.

So when someone tells me of an experience or belief that defies logic, reason, or current understanding, I rarely scoff. I listen, maybe from a safe distance if the person seems to be in need of medication, anger management classes, a shower, or a haircut, but I still listen.

In my experience, there's a fine line between prophet and crazy person. I'm not sure I can tell them apart. When confronted by a potential player for either team, I pay attention. If the person is really a soothsayer, well, I'm interested in hearing how the human story turns out. If it's a run-of-the-mill crazy person on a rant, I believe in being kind and tolerant to them. For me, listening is the way to go either way. I'm not saying I'm comfortable inviting the potential prophet home for dinner, but I still make eye contact, smile, and listen—even if it's from across the street.

I can only say with certainty that I believe in everything—at least a little bit.

Even the most hardcore, non-religious scientists acknowledge that miracles occur. They just call them by another name. When my non-religious friends ask me why I believe in an afterlife, I always explain that I think it is arrogant, close-minded, and self-important to think that life begins and ends with us here on earth.

There's certainly some circumstantial evidence that it exists. Throughout history, there are tales of people who have crossed over and come back or experienced inexplicable, firsthand glimpses into the hereafter. Their stories are remarkably similar, regardless of country, culture, or language of origin. I find that amazing! Maybe it is a mass hallucination, or the opium of the people, or weather balloons that we mistake for flying saucers, but the older I get, the more open I am to living with the unknown, the unexplained, or the unexplainable. I'm comfortable not having all the answers, although I still hope for a fairy-tale ending. I want there to be a happily-ever-after for all of us.

I HEAR VOICES

MY FAVORITE WEATHER IS windy and cold. I know I'm in the minority with that vote. Most people prefer hot summer days. I do not. You need to respect my opinion and move on. I don't expect you to agree with me. I'm not campaigning for cold, windy, wet weather fans. I don't understand why people are so scandalized by my preferences. When I claim to like windy, cold days, people act like I've personally offended them. It's as if I've confessed to stuffing ballot boxes or buying an outfit to wear to a party that I plan on returning to the store the next day. There's nothing *unnatural* about preferring overcast days to sunny ones. It's unusual, I admit, but my preference doesn't make me a nutjob. I'm a little bit tired of having to defend my views on weather. I like storms, too. Big ones. Deal with it.

Where I live, I don't get nearly enough windy, cold days. When I luck out weather-wise, I must hide my delight from the sun-worshipping masses. I check my grin and grumble a bit to fit in with my fellow commuters, but secretly, I'm throwing a little party in my head. I especially like the sound effects on cold-weather days—a roaring fire, leaves spinning across the sidewalk, and the whoosh of wind rattling the last dry leaves clinging tenaciously to tree branches. Those sounds are so much more appealing than the incessant clicking of cicadas on a hot, humid summer night. That is a harsh, repetitive, non-melodious noise that I associate with misery. In fact, that's the sound of crazy in the South, if you ask me.

Prepare yourself. I'm asking you to keep an open mind as you continue reading. I need room to write here, a little literary license, often defined as a willing suspension of disbelief, and some leeway. Humor me for the next few paragraphs, and I promise to give you something interesting to think about for the rest of the day.

To my ears, the sound of wind blowing through trees—that faint, whispery murmur—perfectly mimics the pitch of human voices. In my imagination, these voices belong to all the people I have ever loved in my life who have died or moved away or severed their connection to me in some way. Before you get all worked up, let me reassure you that I've not gone round the bend, I promise. You don't need to call someone to check on me. I can explain.

Automatically, I strain to make out faint sounds when I hear them. We all do. It's instinctive—part of the flight-or-fight decision-making we have built in to avoid danger if possible or prepare to defend ourselves if not. So when I hear the wind rustling the leaves and branches of trees, a sound that seems to be human conversations happening so far away they are hard to decipher, I close my eyes and concentrate. If someone is trying to talk to me, I want to hear what he or she has to say. Maybe this could really happen—who knows for sure?

I want to hear those voices distinctly and to connect with people I've loved who have died. This is the stuff of ghost-hunter fantasies. I've never pursued such hobbies myself, but I'm open-minded. I have been an enthusiastic participant in ghost tours in Charleston, South Carolina, and New Orleans, Louisiana. (That's a whole industry now, in case you didn't know. People will do anything to make money. Humans are resourceful like that. I think it's a loveable trait.) Those were fun. And I had a friend who had a Ouija board when I was young, but we never got any messages to or from the other side. I wanted to stop for a palm reading several times on long trips to the beach with my husband, but I have never been able to talk him into it. He said I could just roll down the car window and throw my money out to get the same result. He's not as interested in being open-minded as I am. I try not to hold it against him, but sometimes it's hard.

Haven't you ever longed for contact with someone who has died, even though you know it's impossible? Sometimes, I think I can hear those people in the wind, as if they are discussing the upcoming SEC football schedule among themselves. It's such a faint sound. The experience reminds me of the time my dentist showed me a cavity on my X-ray.

"Can you see what I'm talking about?" he asked, looking down at my upturned face.

"I think so," I replied, "but it's possible I'm imagining it."

When I feel the chill wind on my face and hear the murmuring, I feel sure that the presence of those voices is real, as real as other conversations I overhear when I'm walking down the street passing pedestrians deeply engaged on their cell phones, or when I make my way past tables of bar patrons in search of a bathroom. When I lie on a beach with my eyes closed, my face turned up to the sun, my body draped across a lounger, conversations around me ebb and flow against the background of waves crashing on the shore. We can all agree those conversations are real. What is so different about the possibility of . . . more?

When I walk across campus on my way to the parking lot after teaching all day, my brain is tired and more open to hearing voices. (You could argue here that my students have actually driven me mad, and I am hearing voices because I'm two minutes away from crazy town. That's one interpretation.) In the minute right before I drift off to sleep at night, I think I'm more open to the sounds around me, too. Voices, maybe echoes of former conversations, seem to crescendo and demand that I pause to remember the random people who have crossed my path over the years. There is no rhyme or reason that I can decipher about the identity of the voices and people that meander across my brainpan like squirrels running willy-nilly across the road.

I know, I know. Hearing voices isn't a good sign. I might be in need of medication or a hearing check-up, but I don't think it's anything boring or run of the mill like that. Don't worry. The voices don't threaten me or give me instructions or anything. It's just a warm presence I feel, like hearing the noises from a fun dinner party my parents hosted when I was a child tucked into bed in another room. It was nice, even then, to hear such pleasant background noise. It made me feel safe and happy. I knew I wasn't alone, and I had nothing to fear.

I believe there are proverbial thin places in the world, spots where this world and the next one are close, literally, as if we are only separated by a sheer veil (think *Harry Potter and the Order of the Phoenix* here), but I believe the thin places may be different for everyone. There is some scholarly reading on this topic if you're interested. I'm not the first person to talk about it by a long shot, which is reassuring, I admit.

When I allow my mind to wander, or when I'm especially tired, that's when I hear . . . more. Have you ever experienced a thin place in your own life? Open yourself up to the possibility. Listen carefully. You might hear voices, too. It's okay. I think we're both perfectly sane. We are in good company in those thin places—in more ways than one.

THE THEORY
OF SMELLS

IT'S A WELL-DOCUMENTED fact that smells often trigger memories in people—good memories and bad ones. That's certainly true for me. I once slept with my husband's T-shirt under my pillow when he was out of town because I missed him, and I'm a little bit of a scaredy-cat when I have to sleep alone. The T-shirt was clean, but I could still smell my husband's unique scent underneath the laundry soap and dryer sheet add-ons. When my kids were little, it was easy to talk one of them into sleeping with me. All I had to do was hand them the remote for the television. Now, I couldn't get one of them to sleep with me if I held a gun to their heads.

I once had a friend who could not bear to clean out his wife's closet after she died because every time he opened her closet door, he got a whiff of her perfume, which clung to her clothes long after she was gone. Each time he steeled himself to get the job done, he ended up sitting on the edge of their bed with his elbows on his thighs and his head in his hands. He wanted to pack up her clothes himself, but, eventually, he let me do it for him. I could smell her signature fragrance, too. It made me cry.

Can you think of examples of memory-associated smells from your own life? Gunpowder. Perfume. Campfires. Cedar trees. Rosemary. Salt marsh. Baby powder. Sunscreen. Antiseptic. We all encounter smells that trigger flashbacks to earlier scenes in our lives. That's a welcome thing if it's a good memory—the smell of a freshly bathed baby, for example. That may be the sweetest smell on earth. I wish I could bottle that smell. I'd spritz my whole house.

On other occasions, smells bring back the memory of old traumas as if they are fresh. One friend confessed that she can no longer bear the smell of night-blooming roses because she was standing in a garden permeated by their scent when she received the news that her husband had been killed. My son says that the smell of an alcohol wipe reminds him of the pediatrician's office and waiting on crinkly paper for vaccinations.

For me, smells trigger highly visual memories. As soon as I smell a scent I associate with a period of time, a person, or an event, it's as though the "play" button has been pressed for a slideshow of accompanying photographs to flash before my eyes. The second my nose identifies a whiff of pine chips, I am transported back to the age of twelve when all I did was ride my bike around a small mill town and read books. I had an idyllic childhood in many ways, and I associate the smell of freshly cut lumber with my peaceful childhood—when my days seemed to run into one another without much disturbance from the adults around me, and there always seemed to be plenty of time to do whatever interested me.

The smell of lilies reminds me of the birth of my daughter. We named her Lily after her great-great-grandmother. Naturally, I think she has the prettiest name in the world. There are a lot of Lilys around these days. My husband bought a huge, aromatic bouquet of white lilies for me while I was still in the hospital recovering from her birth. He also bought a second, smaller bouquet of lilies for our Lily. I fell a little bit more in love with my husband that day. He still brings her lilies for her birthday every year. It's fitting that she received her first flowers before she was even twenty-four hours old. She's the type to appreciate flowers. My advice to boys who come courting: keep the floral tributes coming. She's accustomed to that kind of treatment.

When my sister was young, she told our mom, "You smell so good—just like bacon!" It was probably true. When I was growing up, our house was filled with the smells of home-cooked meals. My friends loved to come to my house to eat. Even now, I associate food smells with homecoming and holidays like Thanksgiving and Christmas.

My children say our house smells like food, too. The reason that our house always smells like food, something I combat on a daily basis with a variety of sprays, candles, and air fresheners, is because our old house doesn't have a vent for the stove. To be honest, I don't think our kitchen is up to code anymore. My children love guessing what's for dinner the minute they step over our threshold, but I would much prefer that our house smell like a spa I once visited thanks to a birthday gift certificate.

The smell of woodsmoke reminds me of fall. I think of swirling leaves, football games, and college sweatshirts. The acrid smell of smoke reminds veterans of something far less pleasant. To them, smoke smells of war. That's a far cry from my happy childhood memories of campfires, roasted marshmallows, and bonfires on the beach. A seemingly innocuous smell to one person can be a trigger for painful flashbacks to battlefields, childhood abuse, or something entirely different for another person.

Experiments where individuals are blindfolded and asked to identify unfamiliar or uncommon smells—aromas beyond universally appealing smells like vanilla, lemon, or peppermint, for example—often produce unexpected results. Because smells are tied so closely to our individual experiences, when those connections are removed or neutralized, people seem to smell the same things differently. What is identified as a pleasant smell by one person may be labeled downright nauseating by another.

Almost every conclusion we humans draw is based on our own conditioning, experiences, and predispositions. It behooves us to know our own triggers and biases. We all have them. It's not necessarily a bad thing. Some people like chocolate ice cream. Others like vanilla or even eschew ice cream altogether and opt for frozen yogurt.

This reminds me of a maxim in law: there is no more unreliable testimony than an eyewitness account of events. Even when all the witnesses attempt to tell the truth as they saw it, under oath, without an agenda, in a sincere attempt to set the record straight, their life experiences, expectations, and prejudices inevitably color their stories to some degree. Each person sees the truth differently and through a unique filter. There isn't *THE* truth, in most situations. There is merely *A* truth. As it turns out, that's true for smells, too. This is a good theory to remember when conflicts arise among friends, family, and even nations.

THE EMPTY COFFIN

I LOVE TO SHOP for antiques. It's interesting to examine curious objects I could never afford to buy nor would ever need—coats of medieval armor, a stuffed buffalo from the turn-of-the-century plains, or discarded church bells, for example. I call it eye candy. Every chance I get, I peruse small shops tucked away in cozy neighborhoods, rural flea markets, big-city bazaars, and school rummage sales. I don't have to buy anything to enjoy the experience, so it's a hobby I can indulge in as often as I like.

I especially like the feel of old jewelry in my hands. It doesn't have to be a priceless jewel. Paste, costume, and handmade creations intrigue me, too. I can enjoy looking even if it's not a piece I would ever wear myself. I imagine the lives of long-dead women who wore each bracelet, message of love, and intricate monogram. Sometimes, I think I can actually feel the imprint of the women on the things they left behind. I have a vivid imagination. It's not hard for me to dream up a different backstory for each piece. Imagine: a woman who died long before I was born held the very same jewelry in her hands.

On one antiquing jaunt, I encountered an item I'd never stumbled upon before: a coffin. The sight addled my brain for a moment. The mere fact that it was for sale amid a jumble of other household goods struck me as slightly crass, unsettling, and a little insensitive. I could imagine all sorts of stories featuring that coffin. Murder. Suicide. A long illness. So many possibilities!

The coffin was beautifully crafted in highly polished mahogany; it was a carpentry work of art. I've never seen that much carving in a modern-day coffin. Bending over the top, I ran my hands across the shiny surface and struggled to read a sterling silver nameplate. The word "Darling" was engraved in flowery script. No other words. Just the sight of it made my throat tighten. In that engraving was the physical manifestation of someone's grief. It struck me as new and fresh, even though the loss was a hundred years ago, at least.

Who was the coffin made for? What happened to the "darling" one? Why was it never used? Or—horrifying thought—had it been used and later *reclaimed*? I really hope not. It's not unheard of, you know. People steal decorative ironwork, marble monuments, and flowers from cemeteries all the time. I have my suspicions about an ornamental iron gate I bought in an antique store. *I* didn't steal it, but I'm not sure no one else did. I hate to think about how low some people will sink when the opportunity for moneymaking is on the table, and no one is looking. I will never know the answers to any of my questions, of course. The good news: there is no "darling" in the coffin NOW. Maybe there never was.

What kind of market is there for coffins in antique stores? Surely no one would buy a coffin on spec—in anticipation of a loved one's final comeuppance. I'm known for being thrifty, but, still, I would only buy a coffin on an as-needed basis, no matter how good a deal I was offered. I have standards.

My guess is that the coffin will become someone's Halloween decoration. The thought of that makes me wince a little. It's the same feeling I got when my daughter played dress-up with wedding dresses we found at a thrift store. Three wedding dresses for less than ten dollars was a bonanza dress-up find, but I couldn't help but feel a bit sad. At one time, those dresses were bought with high hopes for the future. Later, they became nothing more than charity donations, tax write-offs, and dress-up options for a little girl.

A SMACKDOWN
BY JESUS

HAVE YOU EVER NOTICED how the smallest choices we make every day, or the places we go or don't go, or the people we encounter in our ordinary, going-about-our-business days can end up being unexpectedly life changing? If this is a novel thought for you, take a minute and ponder. This is deep. I'll wait. I've been turning this thought over in my mind for a while now, so I have a head start on you. Go ahead and catch up.

I bet you can name a few experiences from your own life where a seemingly insignificant choice at the time resulted in big consequences later, either directly or indirectly. I certainly can. I went through months of infertility treatments before my first child was born. One month, I was told to scrap the cycle and try again later. I remember holding the pills in my palm that would have ended that cycle. For some reason, I didn't do it. It's a good thing because I was pregnant with my son, and he would not be here today. Rarely does a week go by without someone I know telling me a story about a fortuitous meeting or a small change in plans that resulted in unforeseen results. What are we to make of this?

My life seems to move at Mach speed these days. I have three kids, and I'm always either teaching, writing, speaking, or fighting the good fight against steroid-engorged dust bunnies in my home. If I'm not doing one of those things, I feel guilty about indulging myself.

Like you, I work, cook, clean, wash clothes, parent, run errands, and attend to the usual births, deaths, and cultural milestones in the lives of my family and friends, those who are near and dear in my orbit. My regular life keeps me plenty busy. I bet that's true for you, too. I can't be the only person who wakes up tired at least three days a week. Are you nodding along with me and raising your fist in stay-strong-sister solidarity?

I don't enjoy the pace of life in this century. It's true that I've never tried the pace of life in another century, but I'm a voracious reader about other centuries, and, again, I have a vivid imagination. I'm extrapolating here; play along with me. I hate rushing headlong through my day. It may be required of most of us in the modern world, but it's not a natural speed for me. I find it stressful. I know I'm not alone in this because I hear other people complaining, too.

When I load my car for work in the mornings, I see young mothers on my street frantically buckling small children into their car seats. The kids look hastily dressed, and they often have part of their breakfasts still clutched in their hands. Their faces appear strained to me. It makes me sad. They are too young for that. I fear that's what we've come to with this pace: we're stressing out toddlers.

I frequently wonder if I'm losing my mind. Seriously. My brain feels leaky—like an overflowing colander. Because of this hurry-up mentality, I often fail to notice everything I should. I worry that I'm not devoting the time I should to my family and friends. "Always in a hurry" is not how I want to be remembered. I take pride in paying attention to my relationships. Lately, I've begun to fear that things—or people—that/who are important to me are being neglected because I am rushing through my life. How long can I keep all the plates in the air? I don't want to break anything that matters.

At the most inconvenient moment one morning, when my washing machine was overflowing, the cat escaped out the door into traffic, my daughter needed help finding an article of clothing, and my mother-in-law was talking to me on the telephone—all at the same time—I experienced an epiphany, or as I prefer to call it, a smackdown by Jesus.

I'm Southern. Bible-belt colloquialisms are as common as dandelions down here. I've heard them all my life. I like to sprinkle a few in my writing. They add a touch of local color, I think. As an enlightened, politically sensitive reader, you should respect the patois of my people and refrain from mocking me. Feel free to laugh, though. Southernisms are funny. Down here, we know how to tell a story.

I am amazed that some people on national television still think it's perfectly fine to talk about Southerners as if we are all racist, homophobic, uneducated, dirt-eating, trailer-park-living, religious-extremist stereotypes. To be fair, we've given them lots of evidence of those horrors over the years. Historically, it's our cross to bear. I suppose it's the last socially acceptable prejudice in America. Nevertheless, I advise against spouting such nonsense in my presence. I know lots of big words, and I'm not afraid to use them. For those of you who need a translation of my local color commentary, a smackdown by Jesus is the colloquial equivalent of the standard literary term "epiphany."

Epiphany or smackdown by Jesus—either term works for me. Here's what I realized: The seat you choose on a plane, the theater you pick to catch a matinee, or the coffee stand you frequent on a daily basis—any of these random choices can change your life forever. I have a friend whose parents were scheduled to tour the World Trade Center at 11 a.m. on September 11, 2001. I also know someone who met her husband on the side of the road when he stopped to help her change a tire. He got two blocks away before deciding to turn around and come back to help her. To this day, he can't say why he did that.

What if? That's the question. All of our lives can change in an instant—for good or for ill. One phone call with news of a fatal car accident or more joyful news that a newborn baby is ready for pickup by the adopting parents will change everything that comes after in all the lives touched by that one event.

The chaos theory in economics says that there is an inherent order in the seemingly random nature of the world. Just because we can't see it doesn't mean it isn't there. Religious folks like me believe there is a benevolent God overseeing it all, or something along those lines. If I didn't believe that, I would find it hard to get out of bed in the morning.

The meaning of life is a debate above my pay grade, but I'm determined to be more awake to the small, seemingly insignificant events unraveling around me. I believe that the greatest joys in life lie in the most ordinary experiences. I'm going to try to slow down and live at a more enjoyable pace. I'm going to amble, stroll, and pause to catch my breath. I might even take a nap. I'll either finish my to-do list, or I won't. I can live with the consequences.

ASSUMPTION
OF THE RISK

I REMEMBER—EXACTLY—HOW my red, wrinkly, newborn babies' feet felt to my fingers the first time I squeezed them gently in my palms. I can feel, even now, so many years later, the heat from my husband's breath when he bent his head to kiss me for the first time. The sound, feel, and visual from those moments are seared in my memory more clearly than a thousand other more important occasions I've experienced with my husband and children since. Why do I remember those seconds so clearly and barely recollect other seemingly more important occasions?

Milestones like these firsts are common to us all. They are the very definition of romantic comedy, cinematic cliché, and meet-cute scenes. They are highly orchestrated, long anticipated, and fraught with high expectations. They are the high-water marks in our lives that we often look forward to as we mature. I can remember using a bath towel to simulate my wedding veil when I was a little girl, for example, and shaving my legs for the first time without supervision— resulting in bloody, nicked-up shins and knees. We humans are always looking ahead, aren't we? We are always hurrying toward the next horizon. Go west, my son (and daughter, I assume)! These red-letter calendar days break over our heads, ripple out in every direction, and determine the course of the rest of our lives in ways we can't even imagine at the time.

Often, it's the firsts in our lives that define us—a job, a fortunate meeting, or a marriage. Occasionally, however, it's an exit taken or not taken on the way to the airport. We have no idea what the repercussions will be when we live—as we so rarely do except in our clichéd "firsts"—entirely present in the moment.

On rare occasions, it's not the long-anticipated births, graduations, or weddings that determine our fates. It's something totally unexpected that happens with no warning whatsoever. Sometimes, freeze-frame moments of incalculable import come out of nowhere and ambush us when we least expect them. We are driving across a bridge, and suddenly it collapses. These experiences slam into our lives like tornados and wreak havoc in every way possible. There is little or no time to consider, weigh, or debate the pros and cons of decisions made in the heat of these moments.

We have to choose. Right then. Immediately. Between rocks and hard places. We can't call a trusted friend for advice, shout out from the game show cab, research every potential pitfall, or figure out the odds of success in a lab. It's a now-or-never choice that will never come again, a few seconds when a decision must be made to jump out of the window to escape the fire and risk being injured in the fall or succumb to the smoke and flames fast approaching. Should we donate the organs of our loved one or not? Should we jump in the river to save a stranded dog being swept away or watch the scene unfold as a bystander? Will you try to get pregnant now or continue to wait for the perfect time? When is the "right" time to evacuate? Do you stay with the steady job with great benefits you hate or try something totally different?

These are the moments when we are forced to leap off the high dive to see what will happen next. We find out what we're really made of, deep down inside, and what's most important to us when we make decisions under non-negotiable deadlines, under extreme pressure, from deep in the gut, without weighing and calculating, researching, and letting our educated brains overrule our deepest instincts. It's a gut check on the most basic level. Who do you love most? What can you live with or not live with for the rest of your life?

I'm fascinated by these grand moments that come out of the blue. They are small slices of our lives in terms of time, but they have the power to change us irrevocably for better or worse and forevermore. The split second when a choice must be made that will define our personal ethics forever—to do the right thing when no one is looking, for example—declares absolutely who we are, what we believe in our hearts, and what will or will not haunt us for the rest of our days. Can you adopt someone else's orphan? Can you vote for a person you don't respect? Can you forgive a spouse for an affair? What would you say to the murderer of your child? Do you want to live a long life in ill health or a short one that is relatively pain-free? Regular people like you and I make decisions just like these every day.

What makes a person decide in a fraction of a second to risk his or her life to rescue a stranger? What drives another to a moment of infidelity? How does a lone protester suddenly find the courage to stand up to oppressors with no hope of salvation? What is it that drives a wife who has been physically abused for years to suddenly decide to kill her husband? I don't have the answers, but I am intrigued by the questions.

When we die, the legacy we leave behind is the chain reactions begun by each of us in our "first" moments, our gut-check decisions, and the choices we make when we are courageous enough to take a chance—even when it's dangerous, illogical, or a last-ditch Hail Mary pass into the end zone to either win the game or go out in a blaze of glory. For some people, decisions made in a few seconds result in a medal of honor. For others, they result in a lifetime of regret: the death of another person thanks to a drunk driver or a two-second text distraction. There's no going back. There's no do-over. And the lives that are changed ripple out in every direction across miles and generations.

WORRY, WORRY EVERYWHERE

———————— ✦ ————————

WHAT'S WRONG WITH PEOPLE? Has the world gone stark raving mad? I wonder sometimes. Do you? Some days, I feel out of step with everyone else in the world, as if the house is burning down all around me, and I can't get anyone's attention to help me fight the fire or get everyone I love out safely.

Some mornings, I'm afraid to turn on the news to see what has happened overnight. I often feel like I need to caffeine up before I fire up my laptop for the day or check my cell phone for breaking news alerts. Who knows what it will be this time? Landslides, ambushes, earthquakes, explosions, mass shootings, overdoses, and even piracy are such common events that people don't even react to them while ordering their daily lattes because it's not shocking news.

Yes, I said PIRACY! Senior citizens on cruise ships aren't even safe from pirates these days! I can't get over the fact that pirates are real-life threats in the twenty-first century. If I had a child in the Coast Guard or US Navy, I would have to worry about him or her taking on smugglers and pirates like villains from a bedtime story. Piracy is a step too far. It's more than I can handle. What a sad comment on the state of our world.

I envy babies; they never fail to wake up each morning with a smile on their faces. More often, I feel fearful and dread the next tale of horror, devastation, and woe. This is no way to live—anxious, fearful, and worrying. I know that. I confess that I worry about everything, big and small, things I can do something about and things I have no control over whatsoever. I can't turn my brain off. I've had this problem all my life. I worry about terrorist attacks and whether my boys will grow bald and whether New Orleans will finally be swamped by the sea. I guess I don't have to tell you that if you are sleepless some night, you should text me. I'm up. Sleep is an elusive mistress for folks like me. Sure, some of my worries are about things that truly matter, but many of them are silly and self-indulgent.

Some of my worries are well founded, but too many times I make myself sick dreading possible scenarios that never come to pass. When that happens, I am ashamed that I have wasted minutes, hours, days, or even weeks of my life that I will never get back. I write about this subject over and over again, like a stick I use to beat back the panic.

Since I am a religious person, my faith encourages me to be anxious about nothing and to trust in a force bigger than myself, but I can't seem to control my thoughts. I'm a Christian, an Episcopalian to be specific, and I have no trouble believing in God but lots of trouble understanding Jesus as the son of God. The idea of a deity incarnate is hard for me to wrap my brain around. Oh, I can repeat the doctrine in elaborate detail, but it's a lot like when I explain how satellites work or the Internet or physics. Just because I can repeat how it works doesn't mean I really get it. My son, who knows lots more about religions of the world than I do, says that I'm a humanist at heart. Maybe. I'm interested in all religions, to tell the truth. I find it life-affirming how similar they are. I do believe in an afterlife, and I think a whole lot of know-it-all, judgmental, sanctimonious, self-proclaimed do-gooders are going to be mighty surprised by who makes it into Heaven or the next life or whatever. I hope I get to say I told you so and harrumph a little.

I'm a mom. Moms worry. It's part of our job description. I don't know a single mother who does not spend a lot of time worrying.

Here's what I've learned: All the worry in the world doesn't do one bit of good. No one has been saved or even helped by my perpetual state of angst. I've made myself sick with worry and tried the patience of friends and family alike with this tendency.

Here's a little something new I'm trying these days: channeling my worry into physical labor. It's very satisfying. Bonus: it's good exercise and healthier than working my way through a dozen Krispy Kreme doughnuts, too. When I am overwhelmed with fear for those I love, I clean out closets, scrub bathroom tile, or organize my pantry—yours, too, if you'll let me. I would enjoy that. We could drink cocktails and gossip and set the world to rights while we alphabetize your spice rack. Just so you know, alphabetical order is the only way to go with regard to spices. Wait until I tell you how you can organize your salad dressings. It'll change your life.

Of course, this busy work doesn't stop me from worrying completely. It's a little like handing out crayons and paper to inmates in the asylum. It doesn't fix the crazy, but it keeps the monsters at bay for a time. With my new plan, at the very least I have something good to show for my day at the end of it. I love instant gratification. It's a rarity in life.

ANTICIPATION

ANTICIPATION IS ONE OF life's greatest pleasures. Sadly, it is an often-overlooked joy. I'm not pointing fingers here. I'm just as guilty of this as the rest of you. Some people are born with their hands up, gleefully open to the anticipatory joys of a roller coaster ride. My son is one of those people. When he rode in a stroller, he always leaned forward and stretched his arms out as far as possible, as if he wanted to catch hold of everything he saw. He's still like that today. He's one of those people who can successfully communicate with anyone on the roller coaster—even without a common language. Sadly, I am not one of those people. Instead, I'm the person in line for the roller coaster who uses her phone to Google roller coaster safety statistics and then reads them aloud to everyone within hearing distance. I'm not proud of that. Like I said, I wish I were different in so many ways. Sometimes, I make myself tired.

I am more comfortable with the notion of dread. Dread is the mean, ugly, fairy-tale stepsister of anticipation. I am guilty of wallowing in dread. I waste so many days, hours, and minutes dreading an event that looms inevitably on my calendar horizon: test results, an empty/full nest, the loss of a job, an election, a problem at work—life events over which I have little or no control and very little influence. This is not something in my character that others find appealing.

When my kids were young, I often spent the whole week leading up to a beach vacation fearing ear infections that would prevent my children from getting in the pool after we'd paid a nonrefundable rental deposit. That rarely came to pass, but I reacted to every pre-vacation sneeze like my kids might be coming down with Ebola.

The more attractive fairy-tale sister, anticipation, is chock-full of lovely moments—shrieks of surprise, jumping up and down for joy, howls of laughter, hand-clapping enthusiasm, and just plain, everyday, play-in-the-sprinkler-in-the-yard fun. The countdown to holidays or a homecoming is an anticipation cliché we've all experienced, but there are many others, of course. (Are you humming the Carly Simon "Anticipation" song yet? I am. It will probably stick in your head all day.)

I've noticed that I tend to take all the everyday-wonderful moments of anticipation for granted, unless they are "firsts" in some way. My husband filmed our child's first bath like it was a baptism in the Jordan River, but before the week was out, a bath was just a bath. Recently, a plumbing repair finally restored hot water to our household after days of going without. We cheered the plumber like he was an Olympian headed into the stadium to pick up his gold medal. Bath-time anticipation was high that night, I assure you.

One of my favorite looking-forward-to moments is anticipating the reaction of a friend or loved one to a present I am wrapping for them or food I've prepared for them, something I've thoughtfully planned with a lot of time, effort, and expense. I aim to please! Looking forward to visiting with old friends after a long separation, the small happiness that bubbles up when I curl up in a chair to begin reading a newly released book in a beloved series, the excitement of standing in line for an epic movie or a championship sports event— these are the small blessings of anticipation that I enjoy most.

I love the feeling I get right before I step out of a car in a city I've never visited before. When my foot touches the ground, it seems real to me for the first time, not just a spot on a map. I tear up every time I see soldiers kiss the ground when they first step back on American soil. Imagine the longing and the joy of anticipation that prisoners feel when their dreams become reality, and they are finally free again.

I remember every detail of the first time I made eye contact with my children after they were born. I had looked forward to meeting them for so long; that moment was seared in my brain. On my way to the movie theater I occasionally pass the exact spot where my husband first kissed me, and it never fails to make me smile, even though it was long ago. Some highly anticipated moments actually live up to the hype—not all, of course, but some. I love when that happens.

For me, the small joys are the ones I treasure most. I make my living writing about the everyday events most people dismiss as too boring to merit attention. I think "pay attention" is the best advice I ever gave my children—to your friends, family, relationships, and the world around you. Life is in the smallest details.

I am disheartened when I think back on how many hours I wasted in my life—time I will never get back—dreading an event that never even came to pass. The waste of anything—food, work, time, energy, resources, goodwill, money, political capital, space, or anything else that could benefit others—offends me. I want to be a better steward of resources, riches, and blessings than that.

I admit that it's sometimes hard to find something good to anticipate. Poor health, money scarcity, marital woes, and the loss of loved ones sometimes serve as a shroud that dims the light from even the smallest anticipatory joys. But even in the darkest times, every heartache has a small joy that comes out of it. I'm convinced of it. I've seen it happen over and over again. It may take years to surface, of course. Rarely does life work on my timetable. Next time I despair, I'm going to try hard to focus on dread's other, much prettier, more hopeful fairy-tale sister: anticipation.

DIAMONDS, ROCKS, AND ARROWHEADS

———————————◈———————————

WHEN IT COMES TO jewelry, I always choose silver over gold settings, and sapphires, emeralds, and diamonds don't excite me. Unlike most women I know, I would not be happy to receive them as a gift. That's good since I can't afford such baubles, and I don't see any coming my way.

I prefer to spend money on an experience—a trip, a performance, or a museum tour. I also love practical gifts. Yes, indeed, I am a woman who loves a new appliance gift. We exist. I am delighted by presents that make life easier in some way. An innovative knife sharpener and an ice maker are some of my all-time favorite gifts. If my husband offered to buy me a diamond ring or wash my windows, I would run as fast as my legs could carry me to find a sturdy ladder.

I know diamonds are supposed to be a girl's best friend, but I prefer pearls, turquoise, amethyst, peridot, quartz, and jade. I love how all the natural, earthy colors blend into one another with veins of different hues. I like jewelry that has some weight to it, too. I discovered over the years that the bigger one gets, physically, the bigger the jewelry needs to be. Think about it. You'll realize I'm right about this. My wedding pearls, a single strand of five-millimeter pearls, were perfect for my size-two, just-married body, but now I wear a double strand of big pearls, ten millimeters or so, as my go-to jewelry. I hate to think what my jewelry will look like if I keep adding a few pounds every year. Eventually, I'll be wearing bowling balls around my neck.

The truth is: I like rocks. If gentlemen really do prefer blondes like Marilyn Monroe sang in the movie, I'm definitely the brunette foil for her character, the woman who likes semiprecious gemstones, arrowheads, fossils loaded with history, and pottery.

When I was a little girl, my friends and I often tied our boats on the shores of the Alabama River, climbed the banks to freshly plowed fields, and walked row after row looking for arrowheads and bits of pottery and beads. It was a real-life treasure hunt. You can't do that sort of thing anymore. I think it's illegal. Certainly, it's socially unacceptable, like picking over the bones in a graveyard, but I had quite a collection back then—tiny, sharp bird points, long, flinty arrowheads meant to bring down bigger game, large ax or hatchet pieces, bowls and other highly decorated pieces of pottery, and tons of beads.

I love to imagine the lives of the Native American men and women who crafted those items. It would have taken a lot of time and attention to detail to carve bone into attractive and useful tools, to shape mud and clay into food containers, and to select the best bits of quartz, obsidian, and other rocks for arrowheads. All of it had a purpose. The finished products were used for hunting animals, planting, gathering, cooking food, and sewing clothes.

It is obvious from some of my finds that the native Alabamians appreciated art for art's sake, too. The geometric designs I found on pottery shards with their outlines of animals and people, and the sketched-in drawings of trees, leaves, and other natural phenomena, are evidence that humans have always aspired to more than just subsistence living. Given half a chance, a full belly, and some free time, we add an elective: art. I wish more folks on school boards appreciated that. I just read a scholarly explanation that when we began to settle down and farm in one place humans actually worked harder than our hunter-gatherer ancestors before us. We became, in essence, slaves to the land, with less leisure time, harder physical burdens, and poorer nutrition. That research makes me sad.

I still have a few of the best treasures from my childhood. They sit in a large pottery bowl in my living room. I love to run my fingers through them and turn them over to examine them more closely in my palms. I tell my children stories about those arrowheads, and I feel connected by those remnants to history in a tangible way. Sometimes, we need to touch something with our own hands for it to be real.

THE PATHS NOT TAKEN

IS IT HUMAN NATURE to wonder about the choices we didn't make in our lives? Are we second-guessers by nature? I refuse to believe we are all predestined to follow one path or another. I suspect most religions would pass on my membership. I'm a troublemaker when it comes to liturgy. I think we make choices—big choices, occasionally, and a million little choices every day—that determine our fates and the fate of others whose lives intersect with our own.

Who we marry, whether we have children, what town we decide to live in, which career path we choose—those are big milestones we mark with photographs, parties, and speeches. We tend to make decisions like those thoughtfully. Not always, of course—some people run off to Vegas on a whim and get an Elvis impersonator to marry them, and some folks agonize more about which puppy to bring home from the shelter than they do about whether they want to have a baby or not, but I'm not writing about our wild hairs or the outliers here.

Knowing how much we agonize about big decisions—"he loves me; he loves me not" flower-petal-denuding angst, for example— why are we often so unhappy with our choices? If we have curly hair, we decide straight is better. If we accept the boring job with great benefits, later we wish we'd taken the risk and opened our own bar. We often discover quite painfully that no one really knows the "right" thing to do. We all do the best we can with the choices we have at the time, the budget we are constrained to, and with consideration of all those depending upon us. Every decision has good and bad consequences, advantages and disadvantages, and no amount of cost/benefit analysis beforehand will eliminate every mistake you can make. Bad choices seem so right at the time, don't they? That's life. Circumstances change. People change, too. And thank goodness we don't all get what we deserve. I shudder to think about getting what I deserve.

The real heartbreak happens when people feel trapped. The truth is that it's never too late to make a change. Never. People often resign themselves to living in a bad situation, but they don't have to. You can escape a bad marriage. You can quit a job. You can separate yourself from people who bring you down for sport. It's rarely impossible to remedy, change, quit, adapt, run away, fix, repair, give up, confess, move, abstain, fight back, or leave behind. It's not easy, of course. In the best of times, it takes raw courage, hard work, and a detailed plan. And there's no guarantee of success. None of us is entitled to a happy, successful life. First of all, our genes determine a lot. Geography accounts for a bit more. And we can't control politics, economic security around the world, or even unruly friends and family members. There is no instruction manual for happiness. We can't even all agree on a definition for "happiness." And life isn't fair.

Deal with it.

Some loggerhead turtles hatch and make it back to the water. A few of those survive their first swim away from the beach. There are so many "ifs." *If* their mothers make it to the beach to lay the eggs, and *if* they stay buried in the hole, and *if* a predator doesn't eat them, and *if* the tide doesn't rush in too close or too far away . . . The odds are long—for turtles and humans.

Here is my advice: Dye your hair blonde if you've always wanted to. Live your true self—whether that is as a man, a woman, or something in between. Quit your job and follow your passion, even if it causes a big family stink. Surround yourself with people who love you, not people who depress you. If you want a different life, make it happen. You can start with small changes. You will be surprised what a difference one change can make to your outlook. If you hate your work commute, draw a circle on a map that defines the distance you are willing to drive to work. Then look for a job within those parameters. I know this sounds like poster philosophy, but it's clichéd because it's true! Stereotypes exist for a reason. That's how they got to be stereotypes.

If you're a lawyer, but you've always wanted to be a street musician, try it for a day. Pack a backpack, pick a street corner, break out your instrument, and collect enough change and dollar bills to pay for lunch. Why not? If you wished you'd gone to medical school, and it's too late now, join a mission trip and be the helping hands for the American Red Cross after a disaster. If you've always dreamed of going to Italy, learn to speak Italian. At the very least, you can order pasta like a native.

There is nothing wrong with changing your mind and taking a detour from the path you've laid out carefully for the rest of your life. Some of the best surprises come when we least expect them. Don't spend your time wishing you'd made a different decision earlier in your life. Do something about it now. You'll be easier for all of us to live with if you do.

THE PATRIOT

———————————✦———————————

WHEN DID IT BECOME unfashionable to be openly patriotic? Did I miss a memo? After WWII, Americans were showered with flowers and kisses as they helped liberate countries and concentration camps throughout Europe. To this day, America is the first place the world turns to when disaster strikes or despots rage out of control anywhere on earth.

American taxpayers feed more starving people worldwide than anyone else on the planet. That's a fact. We do that. American citizens. With our hard-earned money. Yet, we are often vilified. I wonder what would happen—and I'm not suggesting this is a good idea because it isn't—if we stopped aiding the helpless, defending the weak, freeing the oppressed, or protecting our citizens and others around the world. Would those who receive our aid continue to bite the hand that feeds them? I honestly don't know.

I am proud to be an American. That's not a bad thing; it's a good thing. I shouldn't feel defensive when I make such a statement, as if I am identifying myself so that the rest of the world can hang a target around my neck, but I do. When my son chose to study abroad, my husband and I repeatedly warned him to blend in with locals. It's not always safe to stand out as an American.

I occasionally feel like I have to justify my patriotism to others. I haven't always felt like this, but I do now. When I fly the Stars and Stripes from my porch (a normal-sized flag for a private residence; I'm not stringing up a flag more suitable for the Super Bowl, I assure you), I am sometimes asked by joggers or walkers going by on the sidewalk in front of my house why I'm doing so, as if the custom is somehow dated, passé, or quaint. I feel the need to cite a socially acceptable reason for flying our flag—the 4th of July, Memorial Day, or some other "official" holiday—as if it's unseemly to be openly patriotic on an ordinary day. There is a distinction between being patriotic and being a nationalist, you know. I'm well aware of the difference, and I hope you are, too.

This questioning reminds me of the folks on television who say, "I support the troops!" followed almost immediately by a criticism of our government in general, the country as a whole, large segments of our population, or our way of life in this part of the world. These statements are thinly veiled insults, like the follow-up to "Bless her heart" or "No offense, but . . ."—which, as everyone knows, is code for "I'm about to offend you."

I'm unabashedly proud to live in this country. My hope for everyone else is that they, too, can live in peace and safety in their own parts of the world like I do in mine. That's what we all want, regardless of geography, gender, sexual orientation, religious affiliation, history, government, or any other variable, isn't it?

The success our country and people have achieved isn't some sort of cosmic accident, happy circumstance, or lucky break, you know. It's self-determination that was hard-won initially from King George, and later overcame the loss of over 600,000 of its own citizens in our Civil War and tackled a shameful legacy of slavery, all of which eventually resulted in a country that has ended up on the side of right more times than not.

Sure, our country is still a work in progress. It has flaws, like our record with regard to civil rights for Native Americans, African Americans, immigrants, and gay/transgendered Americans, for example. There is no question about that. But it's still the best place for an average person to live on the planet. I'd infinitely rather be poor here than poor almost anywhere else. When did we become reluctant to brag about that? We don't build fences to keep our citizens here, and there's always a long line to get in.

The circumstances of one's birth do not define one's destiny in this place. Ironically, this is one of the few places in the world where you can legally protest, sue, and generally talk bad about the government and all its minions. We can even re-write our laws, elect new leaders, and continue to scream and rant without fear of death, torture, or being tossed on the nearest plane to nowhere.

Americans occasionally learn the value of this privilege the hard way—by attempting to do the same thing while visiting or working in foreign countries. Not every country can handle criticism. It doesn't take long to figure out that nowhere else is like America. It's the greatest nation-state experiment in modern history.

We often take our liberties for granted, I think. I know I do. We know we will have water when we turn on the tap and electricity when we reach for the light switch. I am reminded of this reality, our "normal," when I see news coverage showing citizens in far-flung places clamoring to be heard, to have their votes counted, to participate in their own government, and to secure the same basic rights for themselves that we enjoy so cavalierly.

It amazes me in the twenty-first century that there are still many countries in the world where women are not allowed to drive, vote, or be educated, where a son is worth more to a family than a daughter, and where citizens do not have the freedom to worship (or not worship) as they choose.

The rights we take for granted are still battleground issues around the world. I can't imagine living in a society where a woman's rape could bring dishonor to her family or where children are conscripted into war. What is considered civilized or acceptable is a matter of where one is born, what one believes, and who is in charge. That's not okay with me. Might does not make right, or at least it shouldn't.

I wonder if I would have the courage of the patriots throughout history, people in every country and every culture, who risk everything to make their dreams the new reality. I am grateful to those from my own country who have gone before me to secure the rights and privileges I enjoy and for those who work to ensure their survival to this day.

When I see our flag, my heart never fails to swell with emotion. I get a lump in my throat, and I don't care how cheesy that sounds. I can easily imagine the desperate faces of individuals from all over the world who searched desperately for a glimpse of our flag to know they were safe, or home again, or about to begin a new life.

SMALL INDIGNITIES

———————◆———————

I WORK AS A nonfiction writer, a speaker on the lecture circuit, a mom, and a teacher at a small liberal arts college. I'm not unusual. Most women juggle more than one job at a time. Our jobs often change every decade or so and require a professional tap dance of remarkable finesse to allow us flexibility to attend to children, aging parents, and all the other hiccups that comprise an ordinary woman's life.

My work as a writer is rewarded with royalty checks, speaking fees, and best-seller lists. I'm fulfilled as a writing teacher every time I hear from a student that I made a difference in his or her life. Teaching is what I do for *fun*. Really. I'm not kidding.

My job parenting three children is a whole different bird. It's a long-term investment. There are no guarantees of success. My children may end up doing time in the big house or joining a scary religious cult. On the upside, one of them might cure cancer or find a way to supply clean drinking water to every person on the planet. Most likely, they'll do ordinary things. That's okay with me.

If you ask a man what he does for a living, he'll answer quickly, usually with one or two words: doctor, lawyer, baseball player, or jewelry thief, for example. But if you ask a woman the same question, she'll stumble around for a bit and then answer with something like, "Well, I used to . . . and now I . . . and I also . . ."

As a stay-at-home mom for many years, I had no retirement account, no health insurance, no sick days, no holidays, and very little respect—even though I believe parenting my three kids is the most important work I will ever do for my family and society as a whole. After all, if I rear children who take care of themselves and those less fortunate than they are—the leaders of tomorrow, yadda, yadda, yadda—I'll have made a huge difference in the world.

When did parenting become something less than important? It's certainly the hardest work I've ever done. The hours stink. The children I live this sleep-deprived, sacrificial life for are often an ungrateful, rebellious, and surly lot. They do not stand around with bated breath waiting for me to impart parenting pearls of wisdom, I assure you.

Just reading my parenting job description makes me tired: short-order cook, chauffeur, maid, laundress, counselor, coach, activities director, tutor, personal financier, world-class debater, and, upon occasion, an independent prosecutor, judge, jury, and prison warden.

Parenting is not for the faint of heart. It's a service, a gift, really, to the world. And parenting isn't a nine-to-five occupation. The big moments come when you least expect them: when you're holding a cool cloth to the forehead of a child who is vomiting in the toilet, when you're waiting in a cold sweat for your child who is late for curfew to walk in the door, or when your kids put you on the spot in public with a question about religion, politics, race relations, homophobia, or any other hot-button topic that makes you examine your own views in a new light.

One of the reasons I love babies is because they are so open to interaction with all kinds of people. They have no prejudices, no preconceptions, and few expectations.

Years ago, my husband and I were eating lunch in a crowded, downtown fish market restaurant. Our son was happily shredding crackers in a high chair and entertaining himself by flirting with a young girl, about six years old, who was seated a few tables away. Over and over, he leaned back as far as possible, made eye contact with the girl, and then ducked his head and giggled loudly in a repetitive game of peekaboo. I remember thinking, *Wow. That flirting thing starts early.*

When I glanced over to smile at the girl who held my baby in thrall, I was just in time to see the hand of the woman seated next to her whip out to slap her viciously across her face. It was so shocking to me that I remember it as if it happened this morning. I could feel the startled reflex of my son before I even dragged my eyes away from the girl and back to him. His screams of baffled rage still echo in my memory. Sometimes, I hate that I have a writer's memory for every excruciating detail.

Because the restaurant was crowded, it was impossible for us to avoid the girl's table on our way out. My son was perched on my hip, and, in a horribly awkward moment, we were forced to pause by the table with the girl and several generations of her family.

The girl's grandmother, I think, took note of my son staring fixedly at her granddaughter, as babies do, while my husband and I gazed studiously at the floor. In a loud voice pitched to reach all of our ears, she addressed her progeny: "I told y'all to stop hitting! That baby isn't used to that. I told you and told you!"

I ignored the grandmother and murmured comfortingly in my son's ear, "See? She's okay." I had no desire to be a part of whatever lesson the grandmother was teaching.

That's when it happened. Before I could pull him back, my son leaned out of my arms and kissed the girl right on her red cheek.

I froze. My arms locked around my son. I said nothing. Not one word. The woman who slapped the girl said, softly, but loud enough for me to hear, "I'm sorry." Neither of us made eye contact.

My son could barely talk, but his reactions shamed all the adults involved in the day's drama into a new awareness. I like to imagine the little girl never got slapped like that again. Maybe the pattern was broken. Who knows? My husband and I were reminded of a different, more insidious, danger—our own reluctance to speak out in the face of the small injustices and indignities of life.

MAMA MEA CULPA

SOME DAYS, IT'S ABUNDANTLY clear I'm never going to be mother of the year. All I can say is that I'm doing the best I can every single day. I'm not a lazy parent, nor have I ever taken the easy way out, even when I have been sorely tempted to be my kids' friend instead of their Negative Nancy parent. I've put my kids first with regard to money, time, and attention. We didn't have a nanny or maid. In fact, a babysitter was a real treat because of the expense. My kids always got excited when a babysitter was coming. We've always had to stretch our resources—time, money, and energy. Occasionally, I've done what I thought was right at the time only to discover later that I should have done something entirely different. I have parenting regrets that haunt me to this day.

Parenting is the most exhausting, heartbreaking, scary, life-altering job in the world. I wouldn't trade anything for the life I've experienced as a parent, but I'm also glad I didn't know what I would have to live through when I first decided to have a baby. I don't know that I'd have had the courage to take it on if I'd really known what it meant to be a parent. Parenting is wonderful and awful, sometimes at the same time and in equal measure. That's the real truth. For me, it has been a job worth doing. I'm proud of the people my husband and I made, and I'd choose them as friends if I met them for the first time today, but that doesn't mean there haven't been bumps in the road. Occasionally, it was a crater or sinkhole.

I find that I return to stories about my worst parenting days often in my writing. It's like a hair shirt made of words. I want my kids to turn out to be healthy, kind, self-supporting adults more than anything else I've ever wanted. Nothing matters more at the end of the day. They are growing up, but the jury is still out on my long-term investment in humanity. They are still works in progress. Aren't we all, in many ways? And I will be the first to admit that I have high standards.

One afternoon years ago when I was baking treats for a school fundraiser, I was interrupted for the millionth time by the excited stammer of my four-year-old, who wanted to know if I had seen the pears on our pear tree. Without even granting him the favor of eye contact, I informed him that we do *not* have a pear tree.

This pronouncement was met with silence and a puzzled face.

"But, Mommy, I see pears," he insisted.

To squelch the inevitable follow-up question, I reiterated impatiently, "We do not have a pear tree! You couldn't possibly have seen pears!"

My son studied my face for a few more seconds and then wandered aimlessly back outside.

While changing sheets a little later, I looked out the window and observed my son and our neighbor in deep discussion. The window was open just enough for me to hear.

"You see those? They aren't pears! My mama said they aren't," my son proclaimed.

My neighbor squinted to see the top branches of a tree and replied, "You sure? They look like pears to me."

"I know, but they aren't. Mama said they're not," he answered assuredly.

I sat on the bed and stared through the window at the impressive boughs of a pear tree so heavily laden with fruit God would have been proud to plant it in the Garden of Eden. Then I went to find my son to tell him how wrong know-it-all grown-ups can be.

The pear story still makes everyone in my house laugh. I've read it to audiences many times.

In my experience, parenting parables get more complex with teenagers. Nothing challenges parents to live up to what we tell our children we believe more than teenagers. My son once brought a homeless man home with him at four o'clock in the morning. His reasoning: we have extra beds and plenty of food. Yep. I love that my son is compassionate, but I was deeply afraid that we were going to be killed in our sleep by the stranger he brought into our house with no warning whatsoever. He's now working for the Federal Public Defender's Office. Makes sense.

If you do it right (up to my exacting standards, I mean, which is a high bar), parenting is, at best, life's greatest challenge. If it doesn't go well, it ends up being life's biggest heartache. It's the biggest responsibility of all. No question about it. Parenting is a sacrificial life in every way—much like the life of a nun. Hard work and good intentions guarantee nothing. Every parent is just one addiction problem, one careless social media post, and one distracted driving incident away from disaster. Rearing kind, responsible adults isn't something I do just for my own family. It helps all the other families out there in the world, too. If my kids turn out well, and they grow up to be compassionate, responsible adults who help those who need it, I think the world owes me a big thank-you note and maybe a bottle of good vodka.

TINY TERRORISTS

---❦---

THE NEXT TIME YOU check into a hotel room and groan when you hear rambunctious toddlers in the next room, your natural inclination will be to ask for another room. I get that. At the very least, you'll be tempted to knock on the door and offer to pay for their night's lodging, as long as it is far, far away from your room. That's an understandable reaction. I've had that one myself. But just for one moment, I want you to think about how hard it is to keep babies quiet.

You can't shame them into it. Babies have no shame. You can't threaten them. You can't bribe them. You can distract them, temporarily, but they may get wound up again for no apparent reason at all. Living with babies is a lot like living with terrorists. First, you have to figure out what they what. Then you have to serve that up as fast as humanly possible—no excuses, delay, substitutions, or prevarication. If you can't provide what they want instantly, or if they themselves don't even know what will make them content, chaos ensues. Count on it. The military have a slang term for this type of mess: FUBAR.

Since my babies are big people now, my ears tune out the fussy, fit-throwing, whining, crying sounds of other people's children, unless they really get out of hand, so out of control that I fear I may have to step in and handle things myself. (I can still do that, you know.)

If my husband whispers to me in a restaurant, "That kid is driving me crazy," my answer is usually, "Not my circus. Not my monkeys." It's an old saying that I recently heard for the first time. I wish I'd made it up myself, but I didn't. I now claim it as my own, however. I'm glad to be past this point in my parenting life—not that teenagers are any easier, not by a long shot.

I ran a tight ship back then. No tantrums. Nice manners. Mind me or else. Like all parents, my kids occasionally confounded me.

One day years ago, when I had only two children, the older about to turn three and the younger about to turn one, I wrangled them into an elevator to head up from the beach to our hotel room. Anyone who has ever attempted this knows how hard it is. A herd dog would have been helpful. I had one child hanging from my hip and my toddler by the hand. He was prattling on a mile a minute, and I was trying hard to respond to every question. I was loaded down like a pack mule with towels, beach toys, floats, cooler, sandcastle paraphernalia, seashell treasures, hats, extra clothes, a diaper bag, and an umbrella. We were all sandy, sunburned, hot, tired, thirsty, and cranky. I was speaking softly to the tiny terrorist in my arms trying to avoid a meltdown before we made it to our room. It was naptime in a big way.

We were crammed in the elevator with assorted strangers. I tried to keep my wet, sandy children to myself, but it was a tight fit. When I leaned down to hear my older child, the baby on my hip leaned over and took a huge bite out of the candy bar the man standing next to us was waving around to punctuate his animated conversation. It wasn't a nibble. He grabbed that Hershey bar with both hands and chomped down on the top half of it. We're all lucky he didn't take the guy's fingers off.

The entire elevator was shocked into silence. Every single conversation ceased abruptly, and all eyes locked on my baby. I held my breath, mentally composed an apology of epic proportion, and ~ited to see how this was going to go down. In the background, my ~ontinued to narrate his every thought about the morning's '·vious to the action happening above his head.

That's when the shoulders of the man holding the candy bar began to shake with laughter. I felt my body relax with relief. It was going to be okay. Thankfully, the victim of the chocolate thievery had a sense of humor. I could definitely work with that.

"I'm so, so sorry," I began, mentally planning a gift basket for his room.

"It doesn't matter," he replied. Silently, he handed over the rest of the candy bar to my baby like a defeated king in battle. "It's good stuff, isn't it?" he asked him.

My child rewarded him with an ear-to-ear grin and a long line of chocolate-colored drool hanging off his chin. My older son reached for the chocolate with a delighted expression. He knew he was about to share an unexpected treat with his brother.

Later that evening, when we went to a restaurant for dinner, there sat the man and his extended family by the front door. Just my luck. He spotted us walking in and immediately began to relate the story to everyone at his table. I smiled, rolled my eyes, and apologized again.

"Don't apologize!" he said. "I like a boy who takes a big bite out of life!"

THE PIANO BENCH

---◆---

BECAUSE I'M A NONFICTION writer, my children have resigned themselves to occasionally appearing in my books. This is not the same thing as saying that they are excited about it. That would be overstating things. It's more like they've accepted the occasional cameo role in my books as a cost-of-doing-business expense for those who live under this roof for free. In other words, they know not to give me any grief about it.

I figure it's the least they can do. My kids are quite happy to spend my writing proceeds, I assure you. Luckily for them, my niche is self-deprecating humor. The joke's on me—*most* of the time. I admit, occasionally the joke's on them, too. I write about what happens in my daily life; they're around a lot, and my orbit is not that wide-ranging.

I don't consider myself sentimental. In fact, it's possible that I take too much pride in the fact that I'm not one of those crybaby mamas who dabs her eyes during a movie, nor have I rained all over my children's senior years of high school because I am sad to lose them to college. I'm not sad. College was the goal all along. Sure, I knew I'd miss them, but I want them to be excited about their milestones—school, jobs, relationships, where they'll live—not worried about their impact on me.

However, I have one crybaby confession. I can barely stand to
ographs of my children as babies, toddlers, and small
ly avoid this activity. If our whole family piles up

on a bed to watch home videos, I busy myself in other areas of the house. It's a little odd, isn't it?

I have hidden all the photo albums from my kids' baby years in inconvenient, hard-to-access hidey-holes around our house like Gollum safeguarding his precious ring in *The Hobbit*. You have to know where to look to find them. You also have to be highly motivated because retrieval involves some climbing and squeezing in between tight spaces. I have deliberately squirreled away photos of my sweet babies. There is no way I can stumble upon them unprepared. I think that is the safest thing for everyone involved. If I accidentally find one of these photos framed on a shelf, pressed lovingly between the pages of a book, or tacked to a bulletin board, I tear up. Nobody likes a crybaby. That behavior is beneath me.

More than I can possibly tell you, I miss the brief time when my children were young and thought I was the most wonderful person on the face of the earth. Now that they are older, that party is over, no doubt about it. I feel cheated, as if I'm being punished for some crime I can't even remember committing.

Sadly, when I look back at the blur of those years, what I remember most are my parenting mistakes—things I wish I'd done differently or better. Logically, I know I must have gotten some things right; almost every parent does. I'd be the first person to reassure another parent who said this to me, but the truth is that my good parenting days don't stand out in my memory. My failures do. They look as bright as the Vegas strip.

I was always in too big of a hurry back then. I saw my role as the rule-follower, the person who keeps everyone fed and cared for, clothes cleaned, and schoolwork done. Be responsible! Be kind! Wear your seatbelt! Take your medicine! Put on your retainer! Do your homework! Hurry, or you're going to be late! No texting and driving! I was always warning, cajoling, and nagging. I wish I'd taken more time to simply play with my children and do fun things. Day-to-day parenting is the hardest work I've ever done. I often allowed myself to drown in the drudgery and lose sight of how precious that time was. It didn't feel precious at the time.

It's hard to evaluate how one is doing as a parent along the way because you're under fire all the time. Occasionally, there is also a sniper in a nearby treetop and fighter jets warming up for a strafing run. I felt surrounded by enemies on many days. Sometimes, I was tempted to surrender.

There isn't much time for reflection or self-examination when you're a stay-at-home parent. Looking back, it's easy for me to see mistakes I made, but at the time, I had no perspective. Also, I was always so tired! I used to dream about walking around the block by myself, taking a bath without anyone climbing in to join me, or going out for a two-hour, wine-infused lunch with my friends. Those were rare treats. My husband and I couldn't afford babysitters back then. For the most part, we either took our kids with us, one of us stayed behind, or we didn't go. We didn't think too much about it. That's just the way it was.

On the upside, I cannot remember a single time when I left my children behind that they cried for me. I often wished they would. Other people's kids cried for their mamas all the time, but babysitters were so rare at our house that our kids got excited when we told them one was coming. They thought we'd hired people to play with them. That's almost true, when you think about it.

One day my daughter begged me to sit with her on the piano bench to listen to a song she'd learned to play. This was not an infrequent occurrence at the time. My daughter likes an audience for almost every endeavor. Usually, I am her biggest fan. I like her. I think you would, too.

"We don't have time! We're out of here in fifteen minutes!" I responded, while simultaneously sorting clothes, packing lunches, clearing breakfast dishes in a frantic attempt to get us all out on time.

"long, Mom, please!" she pleaded.

"FINE," I capitulated huffily, plonking myself gracelessly by her side on the piano bench. I was not patient, thoughtful, or especially kind. I was doing what I always do—hurrying from one job to the next, trying to keep everyone around me in line and on task.

When she realized she finally had my full attention, my daughter grinned big and began playing a fancy version of "Happy Birthday" that she'd learned with a little help from her piano teacher. It was so sweet—a gift freely given to me on my birthday that I was almost too self-important and busy to receive. I can't tell you how ashamed I am when I look back on that day. I thought about omitting this chapter from the book. Of course I did. It does not reflect well on me. In the end, I decided to leave it in. I hope that sharing one of my most humiliating parenting days will help you avoid one of your own.

I made a vow that morning on the piano bench. Never again would I be a mom who is too busy to see a tiny bit of joy in the middle of the daily grind. My kids deserve better than that, and so do I. My kids are all in college, graduate school, or working now, so when they call, I could be having my appendix out, but if they have time to talk, I'm willing to drop EVERYTHING to spend a few minutes hearing about everything going on in their lives, and my standard sign-off to them is "Mama loves you."

YOU'RE SO EMBARRASSING

ALTHOUGH I KNOW IT'S a perfectly normal and entirely predictable developmental stage, it used to really hurt my feelings when my teenagers obviously found me embarrassing. Thank goodness, we are mostly past that stage at our house. It's a stab through the heart that took me by surprise every time, even though it wasn't my first round of sippy cups. It was even worse when my kids rolled their eyes at me, hunched their shoulders to avoid eye contact, or made a sharp about-face to avoid running into me in a public venue like a movie theater lobby, which might require them to engage in a few minutes of polite conversation with me and my friends. To add insult to injury in this scenario, I would have undoubtedly paid for their movie tickets and concession treats.

Just in case you are beginning to wonder if I am one of those genuinely crazy moms who should have a restraining order to keep her from stalking her kids, I want to clear that up right now. I'm just regular crazy—like any other mother of three kids. I have an eye that occasionally twitches from staring at the clock too long without blinking at curfew time, and my clothes are too tight right now, but that's not because I'm trying to look sexy. It's because I'm hoping to lose some weight. If I buy new, even bigger clothes, waving a white flag at my fat and saying, "Go ahead and don't care anymore." At my age, once you give in, there's no going back to single-digit sizes. I'm still putting up at least a token resistance.

It's important to note here that other grown-ups do not find me embarrassing. I asked around, just in case I've been fooling myself all these years. I'm not senile. I'm not unusually loud when I talk, nor do I have any other classically annoying habits, like cracking my knuckles or adding "literally" or "basically" to every other sentence. Incorrectly. I always know what my hair looks like in the back, which is sometimes a good indicator of whether a person is a sandwich short of a picnic. I have observed that individuals who have perfectly ordinary hair in the front and a bird's nest in the back are not as sane as they think they are. Crazy-person hair would definitely embarrass my kids. I can see that.

Furthermore, I never walk around my house in my bathrobe when my kids have friends over, nor do I choose clothing that was obviously designed for girls my daughter's age and size instead of my own. I dress appropriately for my age. I don't snort when I laugh, nor do I have chronic halitosis. As a choir member, believe me, I would know. Any of these unfortunate states would understandably embarrass anyone in my social circle, especially teenagers and young adults, the most delicate orchids on the planet.

I understand that teenagers desperately want to fit in. Except in rebellious moments *of their own choosing*—with freakish hairstyles, body piercings, or tattoos, for example—teens do not want to stand out from the pack. I don't blame them for that. The packs of teenagers wandering the neighborhood look scary to me, too. When my kids were teenagers, I think they secretly feared that some of their mom's far-sighted, coupon-using, seatbelt-wearing, comfortable-shoe-buying, boring shtick might just rub off on them if they were not careful to keep at least an arm's length between themselves and the woman who carried them around in her uterus for nine months.

Bottom line: there's not much I can do about embarrassing my kids if all I'm doing is breathing in and out. I plan to continue doing that as long as I can. I speak politely to their friends, and I hand out cash to my kids like an ATM machine with an expensive hair-color job. That regularly occurring redistribution of wealth thing I do should buy me a modicum of popularity with the masses, but it doesn't last long. An Easter basket or Valentine's Day box of treats that I spend $100 bucks thoughtfully—and thematically—filling and half an hour standing in the post office line mailing for $15.99 gets me a three-word thank-you text. Still, I am determined that they should know how much I love them in the American capitalist tradition. Yep. If their love is for sale, I want to buy it. It's a tried-and-true bribe for ethically challenged politicians, too. Moms like me are no better.

I try hard to blend into the wallpaper when we are out in public together, even when I'm sorely tempted to wade into a discussion about men or women that is clearly based on bad intelligence gathering. It is all I can do not to gasp aloud at some of the things that come out of my kids' mouths. Also, teenagers can be mean. I cannot count how many times I have heard my own progeny declare that they "hate" someone or something.

"That's strong language," I always remind them. "I can't think of many things I actually hate."

"You wouldn't understand," they respond snootily.

Ah, of course I wouldn't. I'm sure teenagers were saying that back in the days when we lived in caves, and parents of the four cave-dwellers that actually made it to their teens were energetically rubbing sticks together to start a fire to cook for their ungrateful wretches—without the help of their offspring, I'm sure. Not much has changed since the invention of fire.

Of course, I know I shouldn't take shunning by teenagers personally, but I find it hard not to. I love them so much, and I long to feel their arms squeezing my neck with their hot, sweaty little hands like they used to when they were babies. Before I became an embarrassment, they hugged me all the time!

They'll come around, my husband reassured me for years, and he's been proven right in the last year or so, but it's not the same. You better believe I hug my mama every chance I get. You never know when a hug from someone, especially someone old, will be the last one you get. In my grandmother's last two days, I went to see her. The family knew she was dying. I was by myself, and when I left, I knew I'd never see her again in this lifetime. I had the hardest time closing the door to the car.

I've internalized that life lesson. I hope you have, too.

I also recognize that the entire relationship dynamic shifts when more than one teenager enters a space. They behave as members of a pack. My kids are much nicer to me in private, so at least I have that—our secret, we-actually-like-each-other-in-private relationship. I can live with that for a few more years, I guess, but it still makes me sad.

At the end of every day spent in the company of teenagers, I reminded myself, *Nobody stays a teenager forever. More than likely, my kids will grow up to be good people who remember at least some of the nice things I did for them when they were growing up*—activities we couldn't really afford to do, outings that took too much time and energy, and disappointments along the way that were hard for us to suck up and move on from. I hope so.

I'm only human. I want some credit when my children are out on their own. I don't need a parade. A phone call, letter, or a single you-were-a-good-mom conversation would do it for me. I could live on that for the rest of my life. I have a note written hastily on a piece of notebook paper by my oldest son from this past Mother's Day that I wouldn't trade for HRH Queen Liz's crown. I have it in my wallet. On my worst days, I can re-read that note and others written by my daughter and realize that at least I did one good thing for the world with my life: I made three terrific human beings.

And, oh yeah, of course my husband helped. Really. He Did. A LOT. But he can write his own book.

MOVING DAY PENANCE

I'VE SAID MANY TIMES that if I don't get into Heaven, and I go to, shall we say, option B, every day when I wake up, God will say: "It's moving day!" I can't think of any worse punishment than an eternity of *Groundhog Day* moving-day repetition. I would lose my mind.

I'm an organized person. I love lists and predictability. Moving days are the antithesis of all that. They are trying under any circumstances, but college moving days are their own particular ring of hell. I'd rather take a beating than go through another one. Really. No head injury, of course, but a few scrapes and bruises, no problem; I would make that trade in a heartbeat. Unfortunately, I see a few more moving days in my future before my kids are out of school, working, and paying their own cell phone bills.

The late-teens and early twenties population is a constantly moving demographic. It's not their fault. They're not doing anything wrong. They're doing exactly what we expect them to do—going to school, getting real jobs, and figuring out how to play a part in the adult world. Moving is part of the plan. Dorms. First apartments. Roommates. Summer jobs. Deposits. Utility bills. Multiple moves are part of the natural progression in this decade. It's a time of constant transition. No wonder this age group is stressed out all the time. I would be, too.

Moving is hot, sweaty work. No one ever moves in cool weather. Never. No matter where the college is located. It's a rule. My kids are inexpert packers, to say the least. I don't think they really know how, and they have no desire for me to teach them either. My suggestions are rejected out of hand like I'm obnoxiously grilling burgers for a PETA rally. My kids always have a "better" plan. They throw everything within arm's reach into a box together, so you have to be extra careful with every single one. You never know what's inside.

Of course, nothing is labeled—even though I've offered my prized box of colorful, differently tipped Sharpie pens. (I love Sharpies. I'd like to scribble a label on teenage foreheads. I could give tips on how to handle them, hints like "feed before talking," "night owl," "needs praise," and "positive reinforcement only.") My kids' moving boxes—and I use that term loosely, since paper bags, backpacks, and pillowcases fall into the category of "boxes"—could contain anything from the crown jewels to empty soda cans and Chapstick.

In the middle of our most recent moving saga, I accidently dropped the box I was carrying up some stairs and discovered it was home to an almost-empty box of Pop Tarts, a handful of belts, a cooler, an open bottle of shampoo, and my son's laptop. As I wiped shampoo off his computer screen with the bottom of my T-shirt, I thought, *I'm too old for this*. It angers and depresses me in equal measure.

I found a set of my son's car keys when they fell out of the pocket of an out-of-season jacket. Those keys were replaced at great expense after multiple phone calls, minor yelling, major inconvenience, weeks of nagging, and serious grumbling earlier in the year. I found new clothes that we excitedly packed before college, which are now stained, torn, and wadded up—dirty—in the bottom of the closet. The hem on every pair of pants has a half-inch ring of black sludge on the bottom. I don't even want to know what that is. Wet towels were sprouting mold in the bottom of the hamper. He could have grown mushrooms or truffles in there.

I came across a retainer that hasn't been worn since the last time I nagged him to wear it, which was the last night he was home, so his teeth have moved back to their original crooked state. All that money and years of orthodontist appointments: wasted. It makes me mad every single time I think about it. I can feel a hot flash coming on right now. I unearthed a textbook that it's too late to return for a refund and cards he never mailed to his grandparents that I bought, stamped, packed, and begged him to send.

The waste, lack of follow-through, inattention to detail, and self-absorption regularly served up by nearly every teenager and young adult I know—not just my own, and I know this because I teach other people's college students in my work every single day—makes my shoulders slump like a defeated soldier. I've taught my children better. My husband and I scrimped, saved, and sacrificed to send our kids to college. We can't afford for them to take for granted any opportunities that come their way.

On days like moving day, I don't think I've done a good enough job as a parent. I'm accustomed to good results from my kids, I admit. They're good students, hard workers, and fun to be around. It's true: not everyone feels compelled to go for the gold like I do. I always want to do the very best job at whatever I attempt. It baffles me that everyone doesn't share that drive. As a writer, I want to be my readers' favorite author. If I worked as a maid, I'd aim to be the maid everyone wants to hire, the woman whose employers throw money at to ensure she isn't lured away to a neighbor's house by a better offer.

Parenting is a long-term investment. It's too early for me to see returns yet, but I'm getting antsy. I find new lines on my neck every day, and I'm increasingly fed up with being in charge of other people's teeth, shots, oil changes, data charges, and clothing needs. I started out as an older parent. It's catching up with me now. I don't know how many good years I have left.

Luckily, I see glimpses of real maturity in my children and glimmers of adulthood, as well. I've been repeatedly reassured by friends who have made it to the other side that most teenagers stumble into adulthood as well as any of us ever did. I hope so. I've sunk everything I am into my mama job.

I've nagged, harassed, cajoled, nursed, bribed, adored, debated, outsmarted, supported, comforted, railroaded, cried on, prayed over, bragged about, been depressed by, impressed by, surprised by, and loved, loved, loved my children from the day I found out I was pregnant with them.

I've made mistakes, but I meant well, and I tried hard. So far, they're healthy, happy, reliable people who have chosen their friends well and stay out of trouble with almost everyone but me. They aren't perfect, of course. Neither am I. When they look back one day on the kind of mom I was, I hope they grade on a curve. I will never be mother of the year, but I think I can hang with the national average. And I hope they learn how to pack a moving box properly, hang up their wet towels, unload/load the dishwasher, refill their own prescriptions, schedule their own teeth cleanings, change the toilet paper roll, call ahead for salon appointments, register to vote wherever they live, mail an actual letter with the correct postage, pay forward a little human kindness with thanks for the many they have received, and that they will feed anyone down on his or her luck—human or animal—that they stumble upon.

ZOO DAY

WHEN MY CHILDREN WERE young, we bought yearly passes to the zoo and visited several times a week. It was a great investment. We sometimes went for an hour right before closing, or we could stay all day. We got our money's worth, no question about it. My children could identify every animal, plant, and zookeeper at the zoo. We celebrated each new baby born there and greeted the inhabitants by name as we walked by their habitats.

Even the zookeepers recognized us as regulars. Sometimes they allowed us to interact with the animals in a special way. They'd often pause in their duties to give us a personal update on a sick animal or share plans for renovation, enrichment, or expansion. We weren't once-a-year visitors. We were hardcore members of the zoo family.

We witnessed the births, deaths, moves, trades, transitions, fights, and dramas of the animals on exhibit as if we knew them personally. We knew where they liked to hide for privacy, how they behaved when they were happy or depressed, and how the weather affected their moods. Sometimes, I think they recognized us, too.

We learned that the best time to view most of the animals was right before sundown when most visitors left, and the zoo came alive in a different way. You could count on hearing the lions roar at that time of day. Other animals emerged from foliage, hidden crevices, and afternoon naps in search of dinner and adventure. To us, the last hour was always the most exciting. We waited near the aviary for the day visitors to clear out so we could be virtually alone with our zoo.

There was always one unexpected encounter—something unusual and exciting—that happened on every one of our visits to the zoo. This unexpected treat never failed to occur; we always chewed it over on the ride home. There was the time my daughter was butted repeatedly by a goat in the petting zoo. Clearly, the goat found her red dress provocative. I actually had to remove her from the enclosure. She was indignant, and I was laughing so hard it was difficult for me to get a good grip on her arms.

Another day we watched the Komodo dragons swallow chickens whole. We watched a kudu give birth, and we saw an alligator take a big bite out of a bird that got a little too big for its britches in the swamp habitat. We fed the koi regularly and once watched another fish jump all the way out of the water and onto the sidewalk in an attempt to get our food offerings.

The ape habitat was our favorite. On entering, we were first greeted by jabbering gibbons. Mama gibbons swung wildly from rope to rope while their babies clung to their backs. The lemurs came next in all their ring-tailed glory, immediately followed by baboons with colorful bottoms, macaques with sharp teeth and furious-looking eyes, tiny marmosets, langurs that looked like they should be climbing the walls of a Hindu temple and, finally, our favorite animals: chimpanzees.

Our chimp families were easy to spot. Their personalities were unique, and their faces were easily distinguishable. They seemed very like my own children in their interaction with one another. They showed affection to one another, goofed around, and threw the occasional temper tantrum, which my children found highly entertaining.

"Sasha is being bad!" my son observed. "Her mama is mad!"

One day, my son, who was strapped in a stroller and parked as close to the chimp enclosure as possible, played peekaboo with a chimp about the same size he was. He used his favorite blanket. The chimp used a paper bag, an enrichment toy given to him by zookeepers. The chimp mirrored my son's every move. When my son giggled in delight, the chimp made sounds of satisfaction, too. It was enchanting to watch. It was spontaneous species interaction. No question about it.

When I pushed the stroller on to the next exhibit, both playmates were furious. The chimp banged on the glass and made threatening sounds and gestures toward me. His message was clear: bring back my friend! My son kicked his feet in frustration in the stroller and turned accusing eyes my way.

Although we humans often see ourselves as far superior to the animals with whom we share the planet, it is good to remind ourselves of our close ties. We're really kissing cousins in every way that matters.

TODDLER TENACITY

———————✦———————

AT A HIGH SCHOOL basketball game I attended, a toddler making her way up the bleacher steps created a riveting sideshow for the home team's fans. I couldn't take my eyes off her. She was clearly a girl with strong opinions. She had obviously dressed herself, and the results were mixed. The kindest fashion review: she was extremely colorful. I genuinely worried that she might cause herself bodily harm since she was walking around on gym bleachers with her shoes on the wrong feet. My guess is that her parents were already picking their battles with her because there was no way you could miss the fact that her toes were pointing in unnatural directions.

The game itself was out of hand. Our team was going to lose. We were down by fifteen to a top-tier team; the gap was widening by the second. The scoreboard began to look like an embarrassing Lite-Brite experiment. It made me wince every time I glanced up at it out of habit. It was a night when, as a mom, my post-game comment would be limited to "Sorry you lost, son. You sure looked good in that uniform!"

Moms learn to work the spin room early.

The toddler attempting to scale Mt. Everest in the gym was the best show in town. She was oblivious to the game but determined to make it up the stair mountain without grown-up assistance. In fact, she *insisted* on independence, slapping at any well-intentioned helping hands extended in her direction by friends or strangers and screaming "No!" at the top of her lungs, no doubt her favorite vocabulary word. It was definitely on the tip of her tongue all night.

She extended both arms for maximum reach, grasped the handrail in the middle of the steps whenever she could snag it, and swung wildly and precariously when the tide of people ascending and descending poured around her. She looked like a salmon with ADD attempting to swim upstream against more with-it salmon headed in the opposite direction at the same time.

The little girl was breathing hard with her efforts and grimacing like a chubby, pig-tailed, big-eyed troll doll with determination. When a pack of elementary school boys ran by her, she reeled back against the handrail, blinked nonstop in their jet stream, and rocked back and forth for a few seconds before recovering her balance. It was a close call.

"Whoa!" she muttered to herself.

She weathered that storm. I wanted to stand up and cheer, but, truthfully, she didn't require an audience, and I did not want to distract her. She was courting a visit to the emergency room all night. She'd set this high bar to please no one but herself. She was entirely oblivious to those of us watching in trepidation. She concentrated on the task at hand intently, and she punctuated each step with huffing and puffing that could have blown down the little pigs' house in the fairy tale.

Each step that she pulled herself up was about half her height. I can't imagine having the courage to take on that challenge as an adult. I'd take one look at a climbing wall like that and head for the concession stand. She was completely undaunted. She tackled each step individually and gave it her all—reaching with arms and legs, occasionally grabbing a handy knee, shoulder, or arm of a fan seated on the aisle, whether they liked it or not, I'm afraid, and she kept her eyes on the prize: the top of the bleachers.

I watched as she reached the summit. She rocked dangerously for a minute on the edge of the top step, turned around to face the court, and grinned with pride at her accomplishment. She looked like a queen reviewing rows and rows of troops before battle. She radiated royal self-confidence and satisfaction over her climbing accomplishment. I was proud of her. I wish I'd had a flag for her to plant at the top. She earned a moment of ceremonial congratulation.

Of course, her moment of contentment didn't last two minutes. I watched as she set her sights on a new goal: a discarded box of popcorn on the top bleacher. Before I could blink, she was off to retrieve her prize. I hoped the box wasn't empty. She did not seem the type to take that kind of disappointment quietly.

I was left thinking about the toddler's life lesson for the rest of us. Imagine what we could accomplish if we approached obstacles like she did. We'd be focused, brave, confident, and, most of all, we'd enjoy the climb. We'd see life as a fun adventure rather than a series of trials to be endured. I'm going to try looking at my next seemingly impossible task through the eyes of that toddler in the basketball gym.

Arms up, people! As wise cowboy Woody says in *Toy Story*, "Reach for the sky!"

STRANGERS
IN THE NIGHT

———————— ✤ ————————

STRANGERS TALK TO ME. I don't know why this happens. I don't think I encourage this behavior either consciously or unconsciously. It's like I have a stranger magnet somewhere on my body. This is not one of my more endearing personality quirks. It's not part of my job to listen to strangers or anything like that. I'm not a counselor or scientist who sees everyone in my orbit as a potential case study. I'm not a dog-collar-wearing member of the clergy, so nothing I am aware of on my person screams out "Confide in me!"

I don't initiate these conversations. It's not me. I swear. My husband worries about this inclination. He fears that I will invite a criminal or crazy person into our kitchen for coffee. I worry about that, too. It's a scary scenario, and I admit: it could happen.

The problem is: I find people so interesting! I can't resist the temptation to make eye contact, and then, somehow, inevitably it seems, conversation ensues. It's like the rule about avoiding eye contact with a toddler who is about to throw a tantrum. Toddlers need an audience for their fit-throwing to be effective. If you ignore it, go about your business, and refuse to make eye contact, you can sometimes cut those dramas off at the pass.

Real people are more fascinating than anything on Netflix or HBO. I can't make up stories more interesting than the tales people tell me from their real lives, and I make my living as a writer, so I'm skilled at massaging a story to squeeze out every bit of juicy detail. Truth is stranger than fiction. That's why that cliché exists. It's also why I write nonfiction. You just can't beat real life for entertainment value.

When I toured the WWII museum in New Orleans, Louisiana, while I was on a book tour, an old man, who was being given a wide berth due to his tattered appearance, bushy ear hair, and obvious need for a shower, sat near me on a bench. When I forgot my vow to keep myself to myself, smiled at him, and made eye contact, he told me about his work as a medic in WWII. With no electricity or running water, he had to be creative to save lives. He claims those were the best times of his life. He never felt as important or useful in the years after the war. It was obvious that he'd fallen on hard times since then. Listening to his firsthand war story made the museum come alive for me. His stories were so exciting that I forgot for a few minutes how bad he smelled. Good storytellers do not have to smell good to be successful. That's just a fact.

Another time, I stood in line for movie tickets behind a circus performer. This is a true story. I'm not making it up. Imagine! I was caught blatantly eavesdropping on his conversation with a friend when we made eye contact, so I smiled in sheepish apology. He didn't seem offended. He was probably used to that since he had such an unusual job. He began to include me in the conversation, conveying tacit approval of my nosy eavesdropping behavior. We never actually introduced ourselves.

I think I heard my husband sigh right about then. He is rarely as interested in strangers as I am, but, honestly, I think he misses out. The man in front of me in the movie ticket line trained elephants for the big top.

"When will you ever meet someone who does that again in this lifetime?" I asked my husband. "How could anyone resist that lure? I'm only human!"

Apparently, elephant training is a lot harder than it looks from the audience. Elephants are smart. The trainer said they have strong bonds within their communities, just like people. I have reservations about the use of animals for entertainment. It feels exploitive to me. I didn't share my opinion with the man in the movie line, however. It didn't seem like the right time.

When I pray for my friends and neighbors, I pray especially for those who are alone. That line in the *Book of Common Prayer* is one of my favorites: "For our families, friends, neighbors, and for those who are alone." I would hate to be alone. I need my family and friends in order to feel happy. When I connect with strangers, I believe that something life-affirming happens—for me and the other person. It's like welcoming a mom from another school to a community-wide event. You may not know each other, but you know you have a lot in common. "I recognize you as one of my own!" is the message I think I'm sending when I meet strangers. There is a yoga theory that explains all this better than I can. Read about what happens when everyone vocalizes together on one "Om" moment.

Not everyone is looking for a heavenly connection with me, of course. I realize that. I confess that my curiosity once sent a fellow bus rider scurrying for another seat. Most of the time, I'm respectful of other people's privacy. Except when it comes to babies. Or puppies. That's Kryptonite to anybody, right? I can barely keep my hands to myself when I see a baby. My children fear I will be arrested for baby snatching when I'm old and senile. They constantly remind me, "Mom—stranger danger!" Unfortunately, to me, nobody feels that strange. I'm rarely afraid, even when I really should be. In my experience, strangers rarely remain strangers for long.

WEDDING HATS

―――――――✦―――――――

A FEW YEARS AGO, I attended my first British wedding in the United States. The bride was half British, so she honored her lineage with a nod toward the other side of the pond. The best part about the wedding: ladies were encouraged to wear hats! What fun!

After being escorted to my pew in the church by a handsome groomsman half my age, which was exciting in itself, I settled in to the sounds of a lively quartet of violins playing an airy, happy, fast-moving piece of classical music that made the hair on the back of my neck stand up and my heart beat faster in unison.

That's when it happened: a wave of joy—pure, unadulterated, champagne-fizzy excitement—swept through the church like a sudden gust of wind from an open door. Everywhere I looked, women twisted their necks right and left, forward and back, in an effort to examine the wide variety of hats and fascinators adorning the straight, curly, short, long—and everything in between—coifs around them. Women practically preened with delight while showing off their wedding finery.

After all, we don't get many opportunities to wear wedding hats in America. It's not the same as pulling a toboggan over one's ears to keep out the cold. Wedding hats are frivolous, feminine, and festive. There are feathers, tulle, and netting involved. You are never too old for tulle. Remember that. You heard it here first. I give you permission to wear tulle all the days of your life—old, young, male, female, or some dress-up-loving combination of genders. Come one, come all to a tulle extravaganza!

At that wedding, I discovered that hats are liberating—much like masks for a masquerade ball. It's not like we can't all tell who the person is underneath the mask; it's just that it seems to grant us a bit of romantic license to loosen up and explore the boundaries of our own personas. I didn't feel like myself underneath the wide brim of my hat. I felt like someone much more interesting and mysterious than my usual potty-scrubbing self. It had been years and years since I was invited to play dress-up. I was reminded of the tea party my daughter hosted for her third birthday party. Hats were required for her tea table, and woe unto you if you didn't have on lipstick, too. Hats, makeup, and attitude are powerful juju. Ask any woman—or drag queen.

All of us wedding guests were trying on different identities for the day. When I saw an old crone from our church three pews away actually smiling unrestrainedly, I almost fell over in my seat. The woman is notoriously cantankerous. She's been in a bad mood for the entirety of the three decades I've known her. It was a wedding miracle on par with turning water into wine at Cana back in the day.

A quiet bubble of happiness welled up in the sanctuary. It reminded me of the giggles that often erupted in the car when I transported packs of teenage girls. I'm not exaggerating just because I love weddings. It wasn't just me feeling the happy vibe. Everyone in the church felt it. It was entirely spontaneous. Strangers made eye contact and smiled. The feeling of hopefulness, goodwill toward all, and dewy-eyed optimism was as contagious as the throw-up virus. We could have been filmed for a movie. It was that sweet.

Guests of the bride and groom felt connected on both sides of the aisle. They weren't avoiding one another like people usually do. They were sharing a moment. It was lovely in every way. We were all in awe to find ourselves adorned like colorful flowers sprouting up in different pews.

That connection among strangers, a result of a short, shared experience, was an atmosphere I've rarely encountered. It was naturally inclusive and worth remembering. I felt it another time while watching fireworks on the 4th of July in my hometown. Families were spread out on blankets and chairs in every direction on Main Street. We all spontaneously sang along with the radio, which was coordinating patriotic music with the fireworks display. I felt it again when I was trapped in an elevator between floors with five other people. We were all a little worried, and nervously intimate chatter broke out spontaneously between people that would have normally avoided eye contact. I was the most worried. I'm claustrophobic. If the elevator hadn't started back in about five minutes, I'd have been reaching for the emergency phone and calling in the cavalry, maybe Quantico hostage rescue. Claustrophobic people don't fool around. The elevator moment wasn't as much fun as the others, I admit.

At the wedding, we were happy to be together to witness an ancient and ever-hopeful new venture for two young people beginning a life together. It wasn't sickly sweet. It was lovely in every way. I love weddings. They are almost always a good day for everyone concerned. Guests are excited, happy to be together, and on their best behavior.

Not always, of course. Sigh. There are some people who just can't help themselves, I'm afraid. I've attended a few weddings over the years that seemed doomed, even at the outset. I once felt like I was attending a funeral for one side of the family. They weren't thrilled about the romance. I have also attended one or two weddings where I was tempted to point out a run-for-your-life, last-chance-to-change-your-mind-about-the-idiot escape route for the bride or groom.

Anything can happen at a wedding. It's a volatile mix of relatives, alcohol, old grudges, petty jealousies, sibling rivalries, work-related power struggles, blended families, exhausted children, pushy priests, hormone-riddled young groomsmen and bridesmaids, and random plus-one attendees. Add a highly strung musician or two, a heated national election, or a caterer with a hangover, and the whole party can go up in flames before the happy couple gets pelted with rice, bird seed, rose petals, or bubbles.

"How can this not be fun to you?" I asked my husband at the reception, while simultaneously eavesdropping on a couple of bridesmaids coordinating their plan to ambush the handsome groomsman studiously avoiding the dance floor at all costs. There was no doubt in my mind that the boy would be dancing within the hour.

My husband shrugged and herded me toward the bar. He doesn't share my affinity for weddings. He does, however, perk right up when the bar opens and it's time for dinner.

THE SCARY
BRIDESMAID

MANY YEARS AGO I was a young bridesmaid waiting patiently in the back of the church for my turn to head down the aisle on the arm of the disappointingly short groomsman assigned to me when I spotted some wedding drama threatening to break out ahead of me in line.

Even though I was concentrating heavily on keeping my bosoms modestly confined in my too-tight bodice, I felt a force field of energy radiating from the front of the church that could only be one thing: a wedding director about to blow.

I nearly snorted out loud when I saw the culprit. No surprise there. The sister of the groom was my least favorite member of the wedding party. No one would have voluntarily asked her to play a part in the big day. There was serious strong-arming involved from the mother-in-law-to-be to ensure that invitation was extended by the bride. The girl was a pill. She was spoiled, petulant, selfish, stupid, and a drama queen of the first order.

She woke up on the morning of the wedding peeved. This was a girl not accustomed to sharing the limelight, and the bride in the big white dress was definitely getting too much attention for her to ignore. She claimed to be allergic to everything on her plate at the bridesmaids' luncheon. When her meal was whisked away and replaced with a sugar-free, gluten-free, low-carbohydrate, all-organic, free-range piece of celery, she suddenly found herself no longer hungry. Even the flower arrangement in the center of the table had to be moved to appease her sensitive nose. She had a list of grievances the whole day long.

When we arrived at the church for pre-wedding pictures, she handed a list of personal photography requests to the photographer. The nerve of the girl! Even the battle-hardened veteran wedding photographer was shocked into silence by her audacity. He tucked her list in his pocket without saying a word to her in response. I'd have gladly torn that list into tiny pieces in front of her face.

I'd been giving her a wide berth all weekend. I know crazy when I see it. When we headed back to the bride's parlor to finish oohing-and-aahing over every little thing, I immediately plopped down on the nearest lounger and kicked off my heels. They were torturing my feet. I'm strictly a flats-only girl. That's when the bridesmaid from hell grabbed me by both hands, yanked me back to my feet, and screeched in my face, "Do you want to wrinkle your dress??!!!" The implication was clearly that my pea-sized brain couldn't foresee the calamity a wrinkled bridesmaid dress might cause. The entire day would be ruined if I took a load off for five minutes, apparently.

I just rolled my eyes in response. It never pays to argue with crazy people, especially those who are about to become extended members of a family that always treated me as one of their own. I'm a Southerner. I learned that lesson early.

It appeared that Scary Bridesmaid had decided to throw down with the wedding director right before heading down the aisle to take her place at the front of the church. I pulled up my bouquet to smell my flowers and cover my grin. The wedding director was an old-money, deep-South, good-pearls-wearing, well-educated, don't-mess-with-me-little-miss, grown-up woman. My money was on her. I knew she could wipe the floor with that girl without even raising her voice.

The bridesmaid didn't even get fully wound up before the wedding director leaned in her face and hissed, "Now, you listen to me, honey.

I've had just about enough of you this weekend. You are not going to ruin one minute of this wedding. You start behaving this instant, or I will peel that dress off you myself and replace you with a cousin the same size as you in about five seconds! Do you understand me?"

There was a full two seconds of stare down. The entire wedding party was riveted. Bets were quickly placed among the groomsmen on which way the drama would unfold.

The result was a no-brainer. For the rest of the day, Scary Bridesmaid was sweet as pie. Always bet on a smart, older woman. We rarely pick a fight we can't win.

THE FAKE EULOGY

WHEN PEOPLE DIE, AND a funeral service is held to honor them, celebrate the faith rites of passage, or send them off with an obligatory farewell party or wake, there are often awkward eulogy moments—regardless of religious affiliation or non-affiliation. In fact, the whole handling of death in America is awkward. Someone DIED, after all. Gone. Poof. Nevermore to be seen on earth. There are bodies to be buried or cremated, casseroles to be baked, wills to be probated, belongings to be distributed, and, hopefully, loved ones to grieve.

I find it comforting that, in our culture, no matter how big of a horse's behind the deceased was in his or her life, there is almost always someone willing to say a few kind words at the funeral. If ever there was a time for kind words, a eulogy is that moment.

Eulogies add a personal touch that is obviously lacking in a service when no one is willing to take on the job. Occasionally, this small kindness requires verbal gymnastics on an Olympic level. Those who have taken on the job have to be creative and work with what they have. The conditions surrounding a funeral are rarely ideal for anyone concerned. It doesn't have to be a perfectly written tribute. It really is the thought that counts in this undertaking.

Nothing is more pitiful than a funeral where only one or two mourners show up out of guilt or obligation. They are easily identifiable because they can be seen furtively glancing at their watches or phones. The truth is that sometimes there is no one left on earth who will miss us. Those who make it to really old age often outlive their families and close friends. Their services would have been impressive if they'd keeled over in their prime, but none of their compatriots who are still around are able-bodied enough to attend. That said, a poor funeral turnout is a small price to pay for a long life. Most of us would take that trade without a second thought.

Another problem is that it's not just kind, generous, laudable, successful, happy, good-to-know people who die. Death comes for everyone eventually. Murderers have funerals, too. So do liars, thieves, pedophiles, animal abusers, and pension-fund embezzlers. Surely, at least some of those folks had moms or dads who loved them, sisters and brothers who played with them, cousins who shared holiday meals with them, teachers who cared about them, or jobs and hobbies that interested them at some point in time.

Unfortunately, somewhere along the line, all that fell apart for them in a big way. That's life. Everyone doesn't lead a charmed existence, no matter how promising his or her life starts out. Jobs are lost. Marriages fail. Friends die. Mistakes are made. Accidents happen. Disaster strikes. Grudges are held. Feelings are hurt. Families, once close, become estranged.

At some funerals, it's only a hired gun who says nice things—a preacher, rabbi, priest, imam, colleague, or friend who has been saddled with the task of eulogizing for propriety's sake. I find it particularly sad when it becomes obvious within the first few minutes of the tribute that the person whose job it is to send the deceased off into the great unknown with a few final words didn't really know the person at all or barely knew the person in the last few years, which may have been colored by senility, poor health, or bad fortune. That's hardly representational of a whole life. What a rip-off.

When the lack of relationship to the deceased becomes obvious, real friends and family members in the audience/congregation make eye contact, exchange wry smiles, and shrug collectively as if to say, "What can we do?" The answer is we can do a lot of things.

There is some glimmer of worth in every human being. It may be faint. Very faint. It may, in fact, be nothing more than a mother's memory of a baby boy or girl, but a final farewell is a moment for the rest of us to reflect on what more we could have done for the deceased in our interaction with him or her while he or she was alive and sentient. Maybe, just maybe, it would have made a difference in the way things ended. Once the final roll is called, it's too late, and nothing, I mean nothing, is more tragic than after-it's-too-late-to-matter remorse.

HOSPITAL
WAITING ROOMS

———————◈———————

HOSPITAL WAITING ROOMS ARE a tiny world unto themselves. When you're waiting in chairs, time ceases to pass normally. It's no longer linear; it moves sluggishly forward while a life hangs in the balance and then shifts rapidly to a blurry, fast-forward gallop when a doctor enters the edge of a waiting room, calls out a name, and hurriedly spews a mountain of almost-incomprehensible-to-a-layperson medical jargon to supplicants desperate for news.

Words like "prognosis," "critical care," "permanent damage," "ventilator," and "potential stroke" are bandied about as if they are ordinary parts of speech.

The emotions among those waiting for life-changing information about the people they love are raw, fresh, and painful to witness. It's Shakespearean drama playing out in real time, a reality show with life-and-death ramifications for all concerned.

The waiting room throws together people who would never otherwise interact. It's a random assortment of age, social class, ethnicity, education, and culture—individuals whose lives have been hijacked by an unexpected accident, trauma, disaster, or criminal act. There has been little to no time to absorb the horrific events that resulted in a waiting room melting pot of simmering humanity.

The veneer of civility is thin, easily shattered, and volatile. Tears flow. Hands tremble. Angry words, curses, and shouts of blame break out. Screams occasionally shatter the silence when bad outcomes are announced in the small privacy rooms. Almost everyone is fearful. You can feel dread in the air. It feels heavy, like high humidity right before a storm.

Waiting room chairs are divided up into clusters of family members huddling near one another for comfort. Children lean into the sides of grown-ups who attempt to project confidence. Adults stare blankly at the floor, walls, or each other. Everyone appears slightly dazed, like soldiers after an ambush.

Almost every waiting room has a crazy person in it, too, someone who shouldn't be there but refuses to be left out of the drama. These people are rarely close friends or relatives, but they appear as if by magic, their presence an invasion of privacy, an emotional drain that no one has the energy to turn away. They thrive on being a part of the scene. They long to be gatekeepers of information, to parcel out news of the tragedy in an attempt to reinforce their own sense of importance. We all know people like this. They're exhausting.

On the upside, there is also a sense of camaraderie among waiting room folk. Small kindnesses are offered—a cup of coffee, the use of a cell phone, or an encouraging smile or comment. I once saw a man offer to move a woman's car away from a restricted area for her. She was in no fit state to drive, and he didn't know her. He had no reason to help other than the kindness of his heart. On another day, I saw a woman take out small action figures from her purse to give to children waiting near her. She didn't know them, but in that moment, she felt connected to them. Everyone in the room is suddenly and unexpectedly in the same boat. It is a collision-style life intersection that easily leaps beyond the normal conventions of getting-to-know-one-another banter. It doesn't last beyond the hospital stay, of course. The relationships are temporary, but the bonds can be momentarily strong.

Waiting-room dwellers are united in hope. They all have one goal: the survival of their loved one and a return to their regular lives. Gradually they realize that from this day on, all their lives will be divided into two parts: before the event and after it. It's a new reality.

LEFTOVERS
FROM THE STORM

———————❦———————

WHEN HURRICANE KATRINA ROLLED through New Orleans in 2005, I watched the news nonstop from six hours away. The twenty-four-hour coverage was painful viewing, but I couldn't seem to turn it off. I'd wake up from a deep sleep to check the news. Then I'd shower with the news in the background and worry about the city and my friends all day long. I thought about how cars float down Magazine Street sometimes when it rains too hard in a bad thunderstorm. I thought about how close Lake Pontchartrain and the Mississippi River look when you drive over the long bridge heading into the city and how inadequate the levees seem when you walk on the top of them and remember their job is to hold back a wall of water from a city which exists primarily below sea level.

I went to college in New Orleans, and I still have close friends who live there. My friend, Gonzo, is deeply protective of those he loves, my favorite thing about him since I know he loves me, even though he might not admit it without being waterboarded. He's a brilliant, mouthy attorney with a sharp-edged sense of humor. His wife, Tricia, is more tactful, but she's an attorney, too—funny, smart, and loyal. In the last few years, they have been especially good friends to my oldest son, too; he ended up at Loyola for law school.

The world is small in so many ways, and social media makes this even more true. I constantly remind my children that everyone in the world is connected, no matter how many miles apart, and this can work *for* them or a*gainst* them, depending on their behavior, so they better mind their manners. Somebody is bound to tell me if they don't. Something we should all keep in mind.

During Katrina, I was afraid Gonzo would try to remain in the city by himself in a protect-the-homestead, macho kind of way. All I could do was watch from afar as the news coverage continued to report what looked like a live-action war playing out on my television screen. There was something almost obscene about it.

Like almost every person who has lived in New Orleans, I fell in love with it during my four years of college at Tulane University, and I never really got over that love affair. If you are a foodie or a music lover—and I'm both—this is mother's milk. It's the city I'd most like to live in if I had a lot of money and IF it didn't share the same latitude as Egypt. That's right. Egypt. And New Orleans is not hot-air hot. It's tropical-rainforest hot. That's a deal breaker for me.

There's no place like New Orleans in the world—the food, the music, the people, the who-dat joie de vivre. Every po' boy, beignet, snowball, and parade I've sampled elsewhere falls far short of the NOLA original, which is downright disappointing, let me tell you.

My scientist friends tell me rather matter-of-factly that New Orleans will be uninhabitable in the not-very-distant future. One of the disadvantages of working with other college professors on a daily basis like I do is that lunch conversations can turn dire over the chicken salad. Professors research and read for a living. They spout statistics and theories that are downright frightening. My learned friends say it's not a matter of "if." It's a question of "when."

The loss of New Orleans would be a tragedy for the whole world. I take comfort in the fact that Venice has been sinking for generations, and only the first floors of those palazzos seem to be permanently wet, but I am practical enough to advise my son not to buy real estate in New Orleans without really thinking long and hard about it. I wouldn't do it. And we made a deal while he's still getting an allowance: category three or higher on the hurricane scale, and he has to hit the freeway.

My friends evacuated their uptown home for what they thought would be a few days in anticipation of Katrina, the usual bug-out that rarely amounts to much, but they ended up being gone a year. With hurricanes, you have time to plan for your family and pets, pack a bag, and secure your property as much as possible against incoming water and local bandits, but who really knows what to pack for a natural disaster? Running shoes? Baby photographs? A can opener? Jewelry? Xanax?

Nobody prepared for a 100-year storm with Katrina. My friends had no hint there would be that much mud and water on their first floor when the gumbo bowl finally spilled over. And don't even talk to me about the levees. Really. I get riled up, and I don't even live there. Take my advice and don't bring it up around NOLA folks unless you really know what you're talking about. You're better off bad-mouthing the Saints, and that's stupid on a spectacular scale. It's like somebody talking bad about the children you gave birth to. It's fine if you do it yourself but asking for a beatdown when other people pile on.

My friends kept the window spray-painted with the giant X attesting to the world that the National Guard had searched the house and found no fatalities. It hangs in their basement. It still gives me chills when I see it on the wall, a testament to how thin the line is between hunky-dory and we're-deep-in-the-weeds territory. We all live closer to that line than we think. We are just blessedly oblivious most of the time.

A slight shift to the east or west, and a hurricane is somebody else's problem. A missed flight, and another mom, sister, or daughter goes down in the plane crash instead of you or your loved one. A delay on the subway on the way to work, and a masked gunman shoots one of your coworkers, but you survive. Fate. Happenstance. Coincidence. Chance. Luck.

Who knows?

I remember seeing a metal plate marking the high-water mark in my friends' house after the storm renovations, but I couldn't recall how high it got when I started writing this piece, years later. It suddenly seemed terribly important that I not forget that detail, so I fired off a quick text to Tricia for clarification.

Sidebar: Friends of writers are accustomed to fielding frantic, bizarre questions. My friend is hard to faze. We're close. I don't filter my words around her. She may be the smartest person I've ever known, and she has a poker face that scares me a little. Advice: Don't piss her off. She's not just a pretty face with a law degree and an impressive portfolio.

Her response was instantaneous: "Four and a half feet. But the important point is that it was *over my baby's head,*" she texted back.

Four and a half feet is just a Katrina statistic, but *over my baby's head* speaks to me on a visceral level and makes me feel suddenly short of breath.

"You rite," I texted back.

If you're from New Orleans, you'll know what I mean by that. If you're not, I bet you can figure it out. Mom-speak is easily interpreted no matter where you live in the world.

COLLATERAL DAMAGE

---◆---

I WAS EXITING THE Fresh Market grocery store with my usual $2.99 Tuesday specials when it happened.

High on bargain glee, I pushed my double-decker grocery buggy, piled with $80 worth of organic, free-range chicken and lean beef, toward the parking lot. In addition to meat, my cart held a prize: a grocery bag filled to the brim with closeout spa products the store was discontinuing and therefore selling at a deep discount, a loss for them and a jackpot for me.

I was daydreaming about stocking-stuffer largesse featuring luxury soaps, bubble bath, lotion, and lip balm—all purchased at closeout prices. I'd hit the grocery-store, spa-day motherload. No doubt about it. Admittedly, I was not paying close attention to the people around me because I was busy calculating my savings in my head. I had to concentrate. I'm not good at math.

The sidewalk in front of the store is narrow and difficult for two considerate, well-mannered shoppers to navigate without bumping into one another. From out of nowhere, a decidedly ill-mannered fellow bargain hunter blew by me on her way in the automatic doors.

She did not pause, slow down, or tread lightly when our paths intersected. Like a guided cruise missile hot on the trail of a terrorist in the meat department, she was on a mission to get in and out of the store as quickly as possible. She was not worried about collateral damage. She was large, in charge, and she cleared the sidewalk like an offensive lineman making a lane for the quarterback.

For a second or two, I teetered in her backwash. Then one wheel of my cart slid off the curb, and the whole caboodle began to list to the side like the *Titanic* about to go under for the last time.

In retrospect, the smart thing for me to do would have been to let the cart go, save myself, and deal with the resulting fallout afterwards. Literally.

Sadly, I didn't do the smart thing. I was convinced that I could wrestle my cart back in line all by myself. I'm surprisingly strong. I can move furniture around with nothing more than a blanket and strength of will. Years ago, I decided to think of this as my special gift rather than evidence of freakishness. Being a strong woman has come in handy over the years. My sons were bigger than I am before they blew out the candles on their twelfth-birthday cakes. Nevertheless, I found it surprisingly easy over the years to reach up, grab a handful of boy T-shirt, and drag them down to my level for a listen-to-your-mama chat.

I held on to the handle of my cart like it was life or death. I was the woman who falls from a balcony in a high-rise apartment building and dangles in the air until Superman swoops in to save her. Truthfully, it always comes as a surprise to me when I realize that gravity applies to me the same way it does to other people. I like to think of myself as a little bit special.

Inevitably, of course, I went down with the cart. It was no elegant, sinking-gracefully-to-the-ground fainting spell, either. I sailed over the cart and slid on my knees for a few feet like I was sledding downhill, face-first, without a sled. I'm sure I left skid marks.

On the way down, I was pelted with packages of hormone-free chicken breasts, freshly ground hamburger, and a tub of pomegranate-infused body butter that broke open and splattered in every direction.

A little old man—half my weight and six inches shorter, at least—rushed over to help. I was not confident I could stand on my wobbly legs, but he put his shoulder into it and shoved with all his might like a bulldozer driver who painstakingly moves mountains one rock at a time.

"Give me a minute," I begged him.

"Are you hurt?" he asked anxiously.

"Pride, definitely. Other injuries to be determined," I responded, completely winded.

"Well, your sense of humor is intact, but your legs are bleeding," he pointed out, his eyes twinkling.

"I'll live," I determined. "Thank you for stopping."

"The woman who knocked you over didn't even break stride," he observed disgustedly. "She was like a tank rolling over a bump in the road."

I appreciated his commiseration, and I have always loved a chivalrous man—of any age or size.

GO AHEAD AND TOUCH

I LOVE BABY FEET. I have pictures of my children's feet—just their feet—carefully saved in photo albums. My kids, whose feet are now adult-sized and much less charming, find these photographs a little weird. I don't care what they think one bit. After all, my baby feet fetish isn't the only thing they find weird about me. You can't worry about polls and popularity contests if you're the mom. I think my kids would rank me above murderers and environmental polluters, of course, but . . . not that far above.

Baby feet, unlike worn-out, calloused, desperately-in-need-of-a-pedicure grown-up feet, are perfect. They are covered in soft, rosy-hued skin that is unmarked by age, accident, illness, or injury. They are bandbox fresh and never before used. Best of all, they still have the ability to head down any path. With a nod to Dr. Seuss, I think, *Oh, the Places You'll Go!* when I see baby feet tucked around a mother's waist. Baby feet are chunky and reassuring when I clasp them in my hands, a perfect handful. I love their heft and how they stick out at almost a right angle from the baby's ankle. That wouldn't be good for walking adults, but it's just right in the pre-mobile crowd.

Imagine having babe-in-arms feet that have never taken one step alone. How wonderful to be passed hand to hand and arm to arm among people who adore you. Babies are so precious to families that their feet have yet to touch the ground. Think about that for a minute. Isn't this a lovely sentiment? No one expects them to stand on their own two feet, literally or metaphorically.

Nothing on earth is more comforting than human touch. The mere touch of a mother's hand on a newborn baby has been known to settle a heartbeat and encourage regular respiration. That's why you see parents sitting in chairs pulled up next to incubators in the NICU of hospitals. Their hands—sometimes just a finger for a tiny, premature baby with fragile skin—stroke lightly on the skin of their babies.

I believe that we are meant to live close to one another and to touch one another, to reaffirm our connections with those we love most in the world by touching them.

I love how kittens and puppies sleep in a big pile. It must feel comforting to them to be surrounded by the warmth of littermates and to hear other hearts beating next to them. Animals need companionship, too. I am constantly amazed that our own pets seek us out to sleep. They could choose to sleep anywhere in the house, but they prefer to get as close to us as they can when they bed down for the night. That's remarkable to me.

When I had three children under the age of five, they often slept together in one bed, even though they each had their own bed. As long as they slept together, they didn't end up in my bed, so I was totally on board with their co-sleeping arrangement. Sometimes my husband and I endured a chorus or two of musical beds before one location won out for the night, and everyone finally nodded off.

The first time I caught my boys balancing on the side rail of my daughter's crib, their toes clinging to the bars like monkeys, in an effort to reach in and pull their sister up and over the rail, I cautioned them not to pick the baby up without help.

"She's little, remember? You might drop her by accident," I warned.

"She wants to sleep with us!" they exclaimed emphatically, as if this were the most obvious fact in the world, and I was just being difficult for no good reason.

"It's mean to make her sleep by herself, Mom," my son argued.

When they continued to tiptoe in and lift her out of her crib without permission, I eventually lowered the mattress to make it easier for them to free the damsel in the white crib safely.

We humans need the touch of others to feel whole, connected, and loved. We all know this instinctively, and yet we forget to literally reach out to those around us—the homeless, the elderly, and the mentally ill, for example. So many people are starved for human touch in their daily lives. In fact, we often go days and days in our households without touching the people we live with!

We are all so careful not to offend others these days by touching them in unwelcome ways. We've become paranoid. We may have avoided some sexual harassment lawsuits, but it's a sad day when you can't hug a student without worrying you will be accused of pedophilia. We sometimes accidentally create new problems for ourselves when we raise our social consciousness about issues of the day. It's one step forward on one issue and two steps back in time on another.

Once when I was trying to load up three small children into their car seats, while simultaneously folding up a big, bulky stroller and also keeping an eye out so no one got run over by a car, no small task, I became aware of a man who parked next to us because he didn't move away after locking his doors.

He stood stock-still and watched me struggle like we were a reality show on television. I felt my blood pressure rise in response. After a few minutes, I made eye contact with him; my eyes said, "Back off, mister!" without using words. He didn't budge. He also did not utter a single word, smile, or offer to help me. It was unnerving. I began to mentally rifle through the contents of the diaper bag in case I needed to make a weapon out of baby wipes and bug spray.

His gaze was intense; his hands were clenched in his pants pockets. He seemed tense and uncomfortable. He was very much invading our personal space, and I'd never seen him before in my life. He also seemed irritated, but I could not see a single reason for his bad temper. I began to get a little mad myself.

When I accidentally dropped my overstuffed diaper bag, he leaned automatically forward as if he was going to retrieve it for me, but then he seemed to catch himself and decide against it.

"Can I help you?" I asked in an exasperated voice, at the end of my patience.

"No," he replied shortly, "I'm just making sure you get in your car without anyone getting killed. You have a ridiculous amount of stuff, but I don't know if it's even acceptable for me to offer to help women anymore. You all seem to take offense at everything nowadays."

I stared. There were so many offensive parts to his speech that I didn't know where to start. Eventually, I smiled. That nearly always works on grumpy men.

"I'm not opposed to a little help," I said. "How about you fold up the stroller?"

"I'm on it," he said. Clearly, all he needed was permission. He became a grumpy man with a mission.

It's easy to get confused about gender roles. I understand that. There are potential minefields everywhere—even for the well intentioned. I'm a touchy-feely person. I rarely think twice before reaching out and touching. I'm quick to hug or pat on the arm. I've found that you rarely offend anyone with an arm pat. I'm going to keep doing that. I think you should, too. Take a chance. Reach out and offer your hand to someone. Dole out a bear hug. Sweep someone off his or her feet. Kiss someone you love who loves you back enthusiastically on both cheeks. Be generous with human contact—even if it's just a smile. Sure, it's risky these days, but what isn't?

UNEXPECTED KINDNESSES

MY PET PEEVE IS unkindness in any form. It infuriates me. I want to wade into those situations, even when they are none of my business, there is nothing I can do to fix them, and, occasionally, despite the fact that they are obviously dangerous. I like to think it's because of my naturally heroic instincts, but really I think it's more a result of my genetic bossiness. I've written about my natural bossiness before. Let's just say it's one of my ongoing character struggles and leave it at that.

On the flip side, spontaneous, unexpected kindnesses bring me to my knees in a nanosecond. They renew my faith in humankind. Just when I despair over some display of human cruelty, I read about a stunningly selfless act that gives me hope. Although we hear horror stories much more often than good-news tales, I believe that such kindnesses aren't as rare as urban legends lead us to believe. They just seem rare because they aren't public events. They're not particularly newsworthy, and they rarely include a lot of people or money.

Ordinary people do good things every day. They adopt or foster children, coach a youth basketball team even though they don't have children of their own, or they take groceries to a neighbor in need of a little help. I have faith in the kernel of goodness in people. I know that sometimes the kernel is tiny. Very tiny. Like a poppy seed. The point is: it's there somewhere. Deep down. Every person on earth has displayed kindness, and even the worst criminals on earth have something more to offer than their worst acts on their worst days. I'm sure even Hitler had a kind moment.

I'm convinced that these kindnesses that go unmarked—acts performed with no expectation of reciprocity, praise, or acknowledgment in any form—make the best case for the possibility of human redemption. That sounds rather pretentious, I know, but I mean it in the most down-to-earth way. If we are all struggling on a daily basis to do the right thing even when the wrong one is so much quicker, easier, and cheaper, isn't that what really defines us?

We look out for other people's kids in addition to our own and pay a little more on our utility bills to help those who can't afford to. We get up in the morning, go to work, and give our best effort, even when we don't feel like it. That's each of us doing our part for good, in my view. I'm a sucker for commercials depicting the pay-it-forward philosophy. I know, I know, they are trying to sell me something. That's a good way to do it. I'm an easy target.

I have a friend who is so innately kind that I envision her being waved into Heaven like she's holding a diplomatic passport at the airport. When she dies, she'll blow through the pearly gates, high-five St. Peter, and head straight for the saints who went before her. I can't remember her ever uttering an unkind word. I doubt she's had many unkind thoughts. I know it's hard to believe. If I didn't know her personally, I wouldn't believe me either, but I promise I'm telling the truth. She's just good to the bone. I hope you've had the good fortune to encounter someone like her in your own life.

A few years ago, she was horribly injured by a hit-and-run driver. Our entire community cried out for vengeance. She didn't. Her view: the driver was probably too ashamed to come forward. He or she knows what happened and has to live with it every day.

"Wouldn't that be awful?" she asked.

I told you she was nice.

I hope she puts in a good word for me with whatever comes next after this world. I'm going to be one of those iffy cases. I like to think

I'm always working for good, headed toward the light, and all that jazz, but some days I'm like an ignorant villager with a pitchfork, rounding up witches and other people who don't agree with me. I often find myself a wee bit disappointing.

Good intentions aren't enough. Anyone can talk a good game. It's the follow-through that matters. A lifetime of small kindnesses— decisions to go the extra mile, make a personal sacrifice, or choose a more difficult path when the easy way is so tempting—these choices will determine our fate in the end. I find that eventuality reassuring and frightening in equal measure.

I've chosen to believe that, deep down, people are good. Just look at all the recycling by the curb on pickup day. That's a small, selfless act. Thirty years ago, nobody thought that could happen either.

IF I WIN THE LOTTERY

I'VE HEARD PEOPLE SAY "If I win the lottery, I'll quit my job immediately, go on a cruise and never come home, or buy a beach house and live it up for the rest of my life!" Not me. I'd open an account somewhere, deposit the money, and just RELAX. The biggest luxury I can imagine is to not have to worry about money.

That's the biggest difference between rich people and the rest of us, I think. It's not the vacation homes, private jets, housekeepers, or pool boys. It's the state of mind. Peace. Confidence. Assurance. Sometimes I think the default position of my brain is worry mode. I'm always scheming to pay for something. Rich people don't live in fear that they can't pay for their kids' college educations, unexpected medical bills, care for their elderly parents, car repairs, or a new roof so that it no longer rains in the dining room during every big storm. For us average folks, the list is overwhelming.

If I win the lottery, I wouldn't change my life in any obvious way. I like my job and where I live. I love my kids and husband more than anything in the world. But I'd love to do more for my children, to fix up my aging house, and to erase the constant frown from my husband's face when he sits in front of the computer trying to stretch our finances to cover one more unexpected bill from the kids or physical therapy or a new refrigerator.

After having three kids who played sports for a big public high school, I can wrap an ankle like an NFL trainer. I also have every size and shape of ice pack known to rehab in my freezer. We even have a nifty ice pack shaped like a human shoulder and upper arm. It's a sleeve baseball players use to ice their pitching arms after a long game with extra innings. It's quite ingenious. I wish I'd invented it. I bet the inventor made a killing.

It's the worrying about money that bothers me most—lying awake in the wee hours trying to figure out how to pay for a new compressor for the wheezing air conditioner, math tutoring, retirement, or dental work that's only partially covered by insurance. Monetary juggling. There is nothing fun about it. It's an exhausting shell game.

Sometimes, I wonder if there is any real money that actually belongs to anyone in the world, or if it's all just anonymous strings of numbers on the computer like Bit Coin. Debits. Credits. Fees. Sales transactions. Investments. Dividends. Bonuses. Profit. Loss. Margins. It's all Klingon to me. In fact, money ceases to be real to me after three digits. I understand hundreds of dollars. After that, it starts to feel like Monopoly money. I often say to my husband, "Those charges are mine, sure, but the total can't be right." When financial experts on television start tossing out references to the national deficit, the GNP, and loans and guaranties, I tune out. Even if their dire predictions prove correct, I don't believe there is one thing I can do about it that will make a difference.

So what I envy about rich people is not the sprawling estates, the vintage car collections, the priceless jewels, or the wine cellars; it's the freedom from worry. My lottery fantasy is the freedom to buy a new stove—something I actually pick out rather than something that will "do"—when the old one breaks without counting the cost or worrying about it. I'd love to just haul the old one to the street, call for a new one to be delivered—without price comparisons, scoping out the sales, or bargain shopping—have it installed, pay extra for overnight delivery just because I can, tip the delivery men a Benjamin each, and never think about that stove again.

That's my repair dream in a nutshell. For the cherry on top, I'd prefer the man who comes to my house to install the stove to be hunky, muscular, and trim. If he works better without a shirt, that's good, too. He shouldn't be too chatty, however. I only want to enjoy the view—nothing more.

Also, if I win the lottery, I'll be a generous rich person. I will be beloved across the land. People will speculate about my identity online on Good Samaritan blog sites. I won't write checks to big charities. I won't endow colleges or build new church buildings. I won't fund charities rushing to help victims of natural disasters all over the world. I know those are worthy causes, of course I do, but they aren't for me.

I'd write little checks to families. If a young couple needed a washer and dryer but couldn't afford one, I'd have one delivered to them, no strings attached. If I saw a senior citizen struggling to pay for her medication at a pharmacy, I'd step up and pay. When I heard of someone who lost his or her job, I'd have groceries delivered and pre-pay the mortgage for a few months. I'd treat a household of troubled teenagers to pizza and a movie, and I'd make sure they each got a soda and large popcorn they didn't have to share.

I know how much it would mean to people who are struggling to make ends meet every month to have just one problem solved for them because I've been in that position. I'd dole out my winnings anonymously, so no one would feel indebted to me. I wouldn't need thanks. The recipients would never know I was behind the gifts, but I'd know I'd done something that day that made a difference in the world.

I CAN WAIT

SOMETIMES, I LIKE TO be kept waiting. You weren't expecting me to say that, were you? Of course, I realize this affinity is unusual. It may, in fact, be un-American to some people. I've observed that many folks have a short fuse when it comes to waiting in line for a present to be wrapped, a prescription to be filled, a runway to clear for take-off, or for a table to become available on a busy night in a trendy restaurant. I've seen arguments break out among strangers waiting for a valet to fetch their cars. Honestly, I am embarrassed for people who behave like that. Adults should have more impulse control than two-year-olds who skipped their naps and got amped up on soda and sugar.

People are so impatient these days! How often is a brain surgeon actually caught in rush hour traffic and forced to lay on his or her horn and run red lights to avoid having a patient die on the operating room table? I bet I can count those uniquely talented surgeons on one hand. Most of us aren't nearly as important as we think we are. If everyone pays attention to me right now and learns this life lesson, I can die knowing I have done my part to make the world a better place for all of us. If the it-takes-a-village theory is true, think of me as the bossy, slightly overweight, nearsighted, menopausal shaman giving you the best advice I've got. I'm trying to help.

Most days find me rushing from one item on my to-do list to the next. I hurtle around corners in a single-minded, grimly determined attempt to tackle my day and force it to conform to my expectations.

I attack my day like a sergeant leading my troops up a hill to attack the enemy's stronghold.

When I stop to take a breath, I often realize how self-important that attitude is. Rarely is there anything on my to-do list that will result in someone dying if I don't get around to it. It definitely would not hurt for me to take it down a notch or two to preserve my own sanity and to avoid driving those around me stark raving mad. I'm organized, a planner, the mom who always has movie candy, change for the meter, paper clips, cough drops, and extra batteries in my big purse. It's a portable CVS store in there.

One thing I hate waiting on: late people. I'm always on time. Sure, we are all late from time to time. That's true for me, too. But I think people who routinely run late are selfish. The message they give the world is summed up by a giant middle finger: their time is more important than ours. I'm talking about people who are always late but never seem to clue in that this is a problem they inflict on other people, and they should leave more time for travel like the rest of us do All THE TIME. Have you ever noticed that there's always a story when they arrive late (and they don't mind interrupting whatever activity they are late to join to tell everyone all about it): I could not find a parking space! The Fed Ex man would not get out of my way! I had to take a phone call!

Newsflash: they aren't as important as they think they are. And if you are one of those chronically late people, shame on you! I mean it.

So when I arrive at my doctor's office, a grocery store checkout line, or anywhere else I find myself unexpectedly waiting longer than usual because I am punctual or even early, I view that time as a gift. In essence, it's free time that isn't earmarked for any particular endeavor because it is wholly unexpected. If it had been pre-planned, there is no doubt in my mind that someone would have found a way to fill the gap in my schedule.

Years ago, my son taught me to whistle when we were waiting for the on-call physician to stitch him up in the emergency department of our Children's Hospital. I don't whistle well, I admit, but I wouldn't trade the memory of his patient tutelage for anything. He kept trying, over and over, until I made a sound that could be loosely interpreted as a whistle. Then he beamed with pride at my accomplishment. He felt like he'd done a good day's work. I could tell.

When my children were babies, we sang songs quietly in each other's faces, read books I always tucked hopefully in the diaper bag, and exchanged kisses and cuddles when we were forced to wait together. My children basked in my undivided attention, and I got to have my day reinforced by baby adoration.

I miss those days. If my kids are forced to unexpectedly wait with me now in an airport, for example, they immediately slide down into their seats and begin texting their friends on their cell phones. God forbid they are forced to make conversation with me. It always amuses me that they tilt their phones away from my line of vision so that I can't possibly read their texts.

"You really don't have to do that," I tell them. "First of all, I'm not that interested. Secondly, no one my age could read the font size you use for texting. I'd need reading glasses and maybe a magnifying glass. Rest assured that your top-secret communiqués are safe from me."

I feel no guilt when I luxuriate in unexpected free time. To me, it's time outside the confines of calendars, clocks, and rigid schedules. It reminds me of the artificial constraint of daylight savings time and the whole "fall back, spring forward" clock adjustment. It's impossible to actually gain or lose an hour, of course. Nevertheless, we've all decided to agree that is exactly what happens at a predetermined hour every year. It's silly when you think about it.

I think the same theory holds true with regard to money. In reality, money is just paper decorated with pretty pictures that we've all decided has value. The minute we, the people, decide it's literally not worth the paper it's printed on, which happens from time to time, the whole monetary system begins to crumble. Yes, we have indeed built our financial system on colored paper.

I often hope my day will contain a bit of waiting in the company of someone I love. It's like winning a round of BINGO, discovering a twenty-dollar bill in the pocket of an out-of-season jacket, or finding a two-for-one sandwich coupon for my favorite lunch spot. A few hours spent waiting makes me less grumpy for the rest of the week.

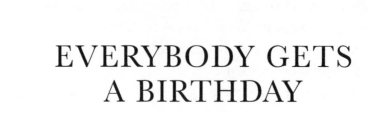

EVERYBODY GETS
A BIRTHDAY

I'M A SUCKER FOR birthdays. After all, it's one of the only celebrations we can all lay claim to. You can't say that about religious or national holidays, relationship anniversaries, or graduations. Birthdays don't have to be earned. It's egalitarianism at its finest. You don't have to be nice, pretty, smart, or interesting to have a birthday. Birthdays are equal-opportunity, unconditional, regularly-offered-up-by-the-calendar celebration days. They aren't dependent upon age, social status, financial security, or geography. They continue to roll around on the same day every year, regardless of the ups and downs of the other 364 days of the year. That's the best thing about birthdays.

When my kids were young, we went all out at our house—big themed parties with lots of guests, cake, ice cream, decorations, treat bags—the whole shebang. I worked for weeks on the party planning and made a lot of things myself because we were always on a budget. I transformed our yard and rooms in our house into castles and forts, and we hosted pirates, knights, cowboys, Munchkins, athletes, movies, games of all kinds, tea parties, bug themes, flower-planting, princess parties, and more.

Now that my kids are older, birthdays are usually celebrated with a special dinner followed by present opening and cake. It's more sedate but no less fun. When my oldest kids went to high school, we actually moved the obligatory lighting-of-the-candle-and-singing-*Happy-Birthday* extravaganza to breakfast. It was the one time of the day I could count on getting everyone together for family time. Take it from me: there's nothing like birthday cake for breakfast to get everyone off to a good start. Carbs and sugar: yum. I highly recommend this tradition.

I hope my kids will remember our family's traditions when they have families of their own. My husband and I worked hard to make every one of their birthdays special. We never skipped one or took the easy way out. Sometimes, we had to party on a shoestring budget, but I don't think my kids noticed. It doesn't take a lot of money to make things a celebration, you know. It just takes the will, planning, and hard work.

I love to celebrate the birthdays of my friends and family, too. It's a great excuse to shop for special treats when I'm out of town for work or on vacation. Presents are something that I would buy no matter what, so shopping all year spreads out the financial burden and lets me indulge in one of my favorite hobbies in different locations.

I take special care to remember the people in my life who may not be remembered by anyone else on their birthdays. A card, small present, baked goodies, or flowers dropped off on someone's special day are especially welcome to someone who has outlived his or her friends, lost all contact with family members, or one who is living far away from family and friends.

If no one remembered me on my birthday, I wouldn't miss the presents, the fancy lunches out, or the parties, but I'd be crushed by the realization that there was no one left who cared that it was my birthday. Take a minute to think about that. Wouldn't you be sad if that happened to you? I bet if you consider all the people in your neighborhood, those who work in businesses you frequent, or former or current work associates, you can think of a couple of people in your own life who may be in that lonely spot for one reason or another. A day might come when that person is you. Find out who has a birthday coming up. Be the person who does something about it.

I promise that you'll be so glad you did.

WHO'S ANSWERING
THE PHONE?

I MISS TALKING TO real human beings on the telephone. I like to hear the voices of my friends. Sadly, talking on the telephone is now considered quaint. I feel a bit nostalgic for the long, late-night phone chats I used to enjoy with friends and family.

These days, communication has zero personality. Mostly, I send and receive texts and emails. They're homogenous. And boring. Autocorrect suggestions from my phone enrage me. I know exactly what I want to say, thank you very much. I make my living choosing the right words. I don't need edits from soul-sucking, know-it-all instruments of technology.

"Talking" consists primarily of a string of one-way messages cast out to friends and family in the ether. Real-time, two-way, interactive conversation between people who devote their whole attention to one another for the duration of the call is a rarity. Such exchanges feel almost decadent now—like the gift of a handwritten condolence note rather than a one-size-fits-all, pre-printed card.

I'm afraid we've lost the ability to engage in civilized conversations with one another. Our children are missing critical lessons about how to read facial cues and body language. I worry that we've created a generation of on-call-all-the-time, socially stunted, self-absorbed hermits. This is nothing less than a crisis in civility!

People are no longer talking to one another. This is a tragedy, and there are going to be real-world consequences. Do you think most of the words uttered by online trolls would be said in a face-to-face conversation between two real, live human beings? Social media rants often read like the journal entries of non-empathetic psychopaths! This is bad. Very, very bad.

In the retail world, I no longer expect to interact with sales clerks. When I happen upon old-world customer service, I'm shocked.

When the clerk behind a department store's makeup counter asked me recently, "Can I help you?" my mouth dropped open in wonder. I was reminded of a time when employees were paid to be nice.

Encouraged by the promising eye contact, I launched into a hurried explanation of my needs. All the while, she clutched her cell phone to her chest like a Secret Service panic button. I knew I was on borrowed time.

"I'd like to try your new wrinkle cream, please!" I announced, a little too loudly.

For a brief moment, we connected. She saw me, a woman in desperate need of crow's-feet erasure. Then her phone buzzed. Her eyes slid away from mine. I watched her fingers race across her keypad as she multi-tasked with customers more important than I.

Every time I have to call about our cell phone plan or some online bill, I fortify myself with chocolate. For every fifteen minutes I remain on hold, I reward myself with one chocolate truffle. (This is my personal incentive plan. You have to find what works for you.) It takes huge chunks of the day to deal with phone trees, music-polluted holds, and online help centers to manage an ordinary household like ours.

It would not surprise me to dial 911 one day and discover that the calls are no longer being answered by humans. I ask you: does this sound like a good idea to you?

"911 emergency. Thank you for your call. Your emergency is important to us. Our goal is to provide a speedy resolution to all your life-and-death emergencies. In order to better serve your needs, please listen carefully. Our options have changed. If you or someone you know is being threatened with imminent bodily harm, press one now. If you, someone you know, or someone you've stumbled upon has already been assaulted or murdered, press two. If your house or car has been broken into, or you've been involved in a non-injury-related car accident, press three, and prepare to wait indefinitely. If you have an emergency not covered by our menu options, press four. We won't respond, but it may make you feel better to know that you have officially tattled on those who have caused you harm. Rest assured that all calls will eventually be screened by an actual person in addition to our fully trained staff of AI helpers. Repeated calls regarding the same incident will only slow our response time. If you are a criminal, crank caller, or someone else up to no good, please hang up now, repent, and go about your lawful business."

SOCKS, SECURITY, AND TRAVELING ABROAD

I WISH I'D WORN socks.

I never do that—unless I'm headed out for a walk or run, of course. I hate exercising, so I don't care how I look in those bleak, pre-dawn treks. Grown-up women like me rarely wear socks in public. Italian, handcrafted, to-die-for shoes do not require socks. In general, socks are a big downer, fashion-wise.

These were my thoughts as I waited in a pre-flight security check-in line in Rome's Fiumicino airport and stared down at my pink, freshly painted toes while armed-to-the-teeth, stone-faced security guards examined my flat, black, ballet-style shoes for hidden explosives.

This seemed like a colossal waste of time. I don't think I could have hidden a credit card in those shoes—even if I were trying to outwit those pesky pickpockets in Florence. Of course, terrorists are craftier than moms like me. Bare feet on public linoleum: that's the new reality for those who want to travel abroad.

As far as I'm concerned, TSA agents can strip me down to my Spanx, force me to throw away expensive toiletries from my fountain-of-youth makeup bag, and X-ray my purse and laptop until the next coming of the Lord if that makes for a bomb-free flight. Aside from some lowbrow Kindle downloads that I'm a little ashamed of, I have nothing to hide.

My flight out of Rome was just three days after bombings in Brussels. Just before that, there was Paris. And San Bernardino, Tunis, Pakistan, and Jakarta. The list grows longer every month. After climbing out of my white taxi in Rome, I had my photograph taken four times before I was grudgingly awarded a boarding pass. Obviously, the new facial-recognition software did not appreciate the fact that I wore contact lenses for my passport picture and later donned glasses for the long flight home.

Over and over, I was called out of line for a special search. Full-body scanner. Behind-the-screen questioning. Counter interview. Even though I knew I'd done nothing illegal, I nevertheless felt my heart rate increase as a tiny buzz of adrenaline hit my system. Illogically, I worried that I'd done something wrong *accidentally*.

"Of course I packed my own suitcase!" I confirmed. Does anyone other than the queen of England have someone to pack for her?

More to the point, if security agents find weapons, bombs, or terrorist-recruiting pamphlets in my carry-on bag, do they plan to nail me for lying? Is that really what's important in this scenario? Surely I'd have bigger worries about the troubling contents of my luggage than a lie I told the Delta counter attendant, a woman who weighed my luggage while I held my breath and prayed that all my shopping near the Vatican and the Campo de Fiori market didn't tip me over the fifty-pound limit. Just so you know, that per-person luggage-weight restriction leads to some delicate marital negotiations.

"No, I can't put your shoes in my suitcase!" I told my husband. "Your size-12 dress shoes could be used to sink a body in the Tiber River!" (I'm still riding the Italy metaphors. Rome is a fresh writing well for me. Did you pick up on the aqueduct pun in that last sentence? Trust me: the ancient Romans could have gotten lead-free water to the residents of Flint, Michigan.)

My hands were wiped with a cloth designed to reveal traces of dangerous chemicals. The zip of my purse got the same treatment. I found myself hoping that none of the twenty-seven products I apply liberally as I shower and dress every morning contains contraband substances. These days—who knows? Sudafed isn't just for head colds anymore.

Meanwhile, my eyes continued to roll toward the five young men seated at the gate whose appearance shouted, "Potential terrorist!" in such a stereotypical way that they could have been used in an *SNL* skit. Nevertheless, the 5'2" suburban mom got singled out again and again for an up-close-and-personal chat with security.

I don't get it. When I try to ferret out which one of my kids is guilty of whatever crime I'm investigating that day, I use every tool in my arsenal and then play the percentages. Sure, I've been wrong upon occasion, but I'm quick to send innocent parties along their merry ways with a cookie and an apology.

Maybe I just look like I'm up to something. I promise you that even on my worst days, when I'm yelling at my kids about less-than-expected grades, their sense of entitlement to every dime my husband and I scrounge up, or their self-absorbed draining of the hot water tank with no regard for those who must shower after them, I'm no threat to the general public.

A CHROMOSOMAL
POINT OF VIEW

SOMETIMES I FEEL SORRY for my husband simply because he's a man. Luckily, he seems equally content with his gender lot in life. If God had made me a man, I think I'd be lonely. It has been my experience that men don't share with one another as easily as women do. Maybe this is how God made us. Perhaps it's basic biology, a matter predetermined by genetic roulette, or whatever clings to the XX or XY chromosomes.

Maybe it's cultural. Sure, men socialize. I've noticed that they talk about work, current events, politics, sports, and their families—to an extent. I'm generalizing here. There are exceptions to every rule. I know that. The biggest gossip I know is male. I'm not sexist. I'm trying to make a point. Follow me down this garden path. I'm going somewhere with this.

Men talk to their wives, husbands, children, colleagues, neighbors, friends, and extended family members, just like women do, but I've observed that, on the whole, they rarely open up to others about their fears, dreams, worries, or emotions as easily or quickly as women do. I'm not making a value judgment. I don't know if this is a good or bad thing. I'm just making an observation.

This lack of public sharing and caring may be a wise move on their part. I've certainly regretted befriending an oddball or two, but I've also shared some interesting experiences with women

I've barely met, just because we survived a three-car pileup at an intersection together, used the same hair salon, or been assigned cleanup duty together after a middle school dance. You bond quickly with a woman when you have to go through the cafeteria garbage cans to search for a lost retainer together. It doesn't make sense to stand on ceremony with someone who is hands-deep with you in half-eaten peanut butter sandwiches and chocolate pudding cups. If there is a more obvious lay-it-all-out-there moment than that, I can't imagine what it would be.

While I was waiting in a hair salon recently for my color to sink in, the woman seated next to me, someone I'd never laid eyes on in my life before that moment, spoke to me in worry-laden whispers about her misbehaving teens and her struggles with a difficult coworker. We used our time together to strategize about ways to address her coworker problems and commiserate about the trials of rearing teenagers without losing our minds.

It wasn't awkward at all. It seemed perfectly natural to me—a wise use of our time waiting with hair dye on our heads. When I told my husband about it later, he seemed appalled, like I'd held a prayer vigil in the parking lot, asked to see someone's appendectomy scar, or demanded that a woman identify her baby daddy.

The woman in the salon left a little stronger, I think. She was fortified by our brief interaction. I left with a recipe she swears will dazzle my next dinner party guests. That's a win-win encounter between strangers, no matter how you look at it.

If we were male, I doubt we'd have spoken to one another while we were waiting. I might have offered her a tissue when I saw tears in her eyes; that's something my husband would do, but we wouldn't have had a heart-to-heart chat. She would have continued to worry needlessly about her daughter's typical teen behavior, an experience I've already lived through and could help her with, and I wouldn't have learned the secret to releasing a cheesecake from a springform pan, a neat trick I've never mastered until now.

We were both better off after sharing. Grief, loneliness, anger, pain, marital problems, guilt, or depression—you name the drama, and odds are that someone you know has experienced the exact same trouble you're in and found a way to hack through the jungle and get to the fresh water source. None of us is as unique and special as we think we are. The old Ecclesiastes quote is true: there's not much new under the sun.

I'm not so naïve as to suggest that these brief interactions will change someone's life in a profound way or that trouble will magically vanish in a puff of smoke. That rarely happens in the real world. What I'm talking about is perspective, sympathy, common experiences, understanding, problem-solving, burden-sharing, momentary distractions, practical help, good advice, wise counsel, and, occasionally, a well-placed kick in the rear.

That's how women help one another out. When I think about this talent, it makes me proud of my gender. This is what being a feminist means to me. I'm proud to be one, and I've reared children—boys and girls—who are, too. We really should pat ourselves on the back more.

SHARING THE MIRROR

———————✦———————

ONE MORNING AS I frantically rushed through my early morning get-everyone-dressed-and-out-the-door-on-time routine, my husband, who is usually halfway to work by that time of the day, and I were forced to share a bathroom mirror. It's a big mirror but still too intimate for two busy people who have yet to be caffeinated. In any event, my hairspray bottle and I need room to move and groove. My husband is a big guy; he takes up a lot of space. We rarely double up in the bathroom. It's true that we use the same bathroom all the time, but we always take turns. There's a difference, and it's an important distinction.

People who have been married as long as we have are shaking their heads at my foolishness. They know bathroom sharing is the first step toward divorce court. Don't get me wrong: I'm not saying that you have to have more than one bathroom in your house to remain happily married. That's not the case at all. The secret to harmony is this: you can't use the facilities at the same time.

The problem on this particular morning was that my husband was helping me. He woke up early, had some flexibility in his morning schedule, and he was trying to be a nice guy. As a result of his well-intentioned help, it took me twice as long as usual to dress and start my day. I have my morning prep down to a finely tuned ritual. I've been refining it since I was twelve years old. I don't need suggestions for improvement from an amateur who doesn't even wear makeup, contact lenses, or use product in his hair. For goodness sake, I think the man still washes his face with soap. If I did that, my face would instantly shrivel up like a raisin.

On my calendar for the day was a noon speaking event about an hour away. Speaking is my favorite part of my job as an author. I love meeting new readers, and the food at such events is usually top shelf. Even if it isn't, because I do not have to shop for it, cook it, or clean up afterwards, I'm still golden. Mama writers like me are not hard to please. My speaking gigs feel like luncheon or dinner dates with friends. As far as I'm concerned, it's just plain fun. Bonus: I get paid to do it! Although I've done it hundreds of times over the years, I'm still shocked that people pay me real money to run my mouth. I don't think anyone on earth has a better job than I do, at least regarding the speaking part of my jobs. I'm a woman. I have at least three additional jobs as a writer, teacher, and parent.

As the designated entertainment for events, I always try to look as appealing as I can. Some days it is harder to make that happen than others. I can't pull off just any old outfit anymore like I did when I was younger. On the plus side, I can afford nicer clothes now, so it evens out, I think. I feel more pressure to look attractive and be on my best behavior when I'm the speaker than I do if I'm merely an attendee. It's like being the birthday girl at the birthday party. Although I want my work to appear spontaneous and effortless to every person in the room, it isn't. I'm a professional; I work hard at what I do, and I take my work seriously.

For the period of time my services have been booked, I consider the organization that pays me to be my boss. I'm happy for them to utilize me however they see fit, as long as it's legal, safe, and not too unseemly. Safe, sane, and consensual—I think that rule applies nicely to writing gigs as well as sexual adventures. I will schmooze with fundraisers, have my picture taken with readers, answer questions, and accommodate as many signing requests as possible from the crowd. It's fun to be the guest of honor, although I'm relieved that guest speakers aren't given mother-of-the-bride corsages to wear these days. They make me look fat.

While staring in the mirror and attempting to coax my hair into an acceptable level of appearing-in-public curliness, I made the mistake of talking to myself out loud. I bemoaned the fact that my hair needed a cut-and-color job in the worst way.

My mistake was whining out loud about my plight. I should definitely know better by now. Like always, my husband then mistakenly assumed I had just made a request of him. One of his self-assigned jobs is to get whatever it is I say I want, to make suggestions about how I should solve a problem myself, or to generally give wise counsel. In other words, he tried to fix my problem. As a judge, his advice is regularly solicited, so giving advice is in his actual job as well as his natural inclination as a nice guy.

I know what you're thinking: "I cannot believe this woman has the audacity to complain about a husband whose mission in life is to solve her problems!" I know it sounds bad. Let me explain.

I love that if I say I feel like eating a steak, my husband immediately runs out of the mouth of the cave, bonks something over the head, and drags it back to grill out. I appreciate the fact that if I asked him to hang a painting upside down for me in the living room, I'm convinced he'd do it with very few questions. He doesn't care what I hang in the living room, and he wants me to be happy. This philosophy works for me in a big way most of the time. However, sometimes, as in this case, I don't need him to do anything at all. I had it under control. I was merely venting rhetorically to my reflection in the mirror. He just happened to be standing next to me because we were *sharing the bathroom mirror.*

"Why don't you run by and get a trim on the way to your event?" he suggested, as if this were actually a real option.

"I don't get my hair cut at a barber shop, sweetie. It doesn't work that way in a salon," I educated him. "I'll just rant about how much I need to get my hair done in the speech. The audience will laugh. They've all been there."

"You're going to talk about your hair at a work event?" my husband asked, visibly shocked. "That sounds so unprofessional. Thank God men don't talk about stuff like that." He looked a little shaken. "I don't know what I'd say if somebody asked me about my haircut in the middle of a meeting. That's so personal."

This revelation did not surprise me.

"I'm not sure I really understand what you talk about when you speak," my husband continued to muse, leaning against the bathroom counter. "I've seen you do it, but it still doesn't always make sense to me." His arms were crossed, and he eyed me speculatively over the top of his reading glasses. After many years of marriage, he was still trying to figure me out.

I laughed. The man spoke the truth. He has no idea how my work world works. His is very different. I think he secretly thinks I make things up like I'm writing for daytime television. I feel the same way when he describes some of the antics judges and lawyers get up to. Lord have mercy. I've concluded that a little mystery is a good thing in a marriage, and I'm pleased to know I can occasionally still surprise my husband.

THE
TREACHEROUS SCALE

ONE MORNING I WOKE up in my own bed, took a shower, and weighed myself on my bathroom scale, as usual. That's all part of my usual routine. As expected, my weight was not a delightful, surprising throwback to the svelte number of a decade or so ago, but it wasn't an all-time high, either. It was the usual. I should lose ten pounds immediately; more would be better.

I then did what I always do. I made a face at my feet and briefly considered the advantages and disadvantages of the numerous diets I've tried over the last few years. Every diet works, you know—for a while.

I want to lose weight and get back into my favorite pair of jeans. Definitely. I also want to eat and drink whatever I want with my friends without gaining weight. I was able to do that for the first forty-five years of my life. It was great. Then, out of the blue, I began to gain weight when I simply looked at birthday cake through a bakery store window. I'm not kidding. I think I may be taking in calories through my eyeballs. Somebody needs to look into that. It might be a thing.

After dressing, my husband and I were off for a romantic getaway. Really, we had to pick up our daughter from camp, so spending the night in a hotel was already in the budget. We decided to upgrade the stay and turn it into an anniversary night. We're good at double dipping.

That night, we walked around the city, had drinks on the rooftop of the hotel by the pool, enjoyed one of our favorite restaurants within walking distance of our historic, luxurious hotel, and then finished the night downstairs in the piano bar. We know the pianist, so he started playing one of our favorites when we walked in the door from the street. It was one of those effortless evenings where everything falls into place without any pre-planning. I felt like a woman on a date. In a movie. Twenty-four hours is about all we can afford to live in the land of the rich and famous without skimming off the college funds, so a one-night hotel retreat is perfect for us.

I woke up after a night of uninterrupted sleep, spent an hour reading in the hotel's decadent soaker tub, and felt benevolent toward the world.

That euphoria didn't last long. When I reached under the bathroom counter for a towel, I noticed a clear glass, minimalist-style bathroom scale tucked discreetly away. Of course, I had to try it out.

That's when I discovered that I had gained sixteen pounds overnight. Sixteen pounds. No way! Isn't that metabolically impossible? I screamed for my husband to weigh himself on the paper-thin, snarky, digital, uber-modern scale to see if my result was a fluke. He made me leave the bathroom before he stepped up to the judgmental piece of hardware. We don't share exact numbers when it comes to weight. Nobody but me needs to know exactly how much I weigh. I have a friend, Barbara, who doesn't even share that information with her doctor. When a nurse asks her to step on the scale, she says, "I don't think I will, thank you." She's a formidable Southern woman. I think the nurses are too scared of her to insist. Wise of them. She scares me, too, and I'm fairly formidable myself.

The bathroom door opened. "Seems okay to me," he replied, his eyes downcast. He refused to make eye contact with me, the fit-throwing harpy he knew I could morph into at any moment. "It could be a little off, though."

"There is NO WAY that scale is right!" I screeched, my voice heading straight up two octaves. "I simply cannot live in a world where I gain sixteen pounds while I sleep! It's too much! I can't worry about terrorism, my children texting and driving, whether or not mole removal is covered by health insurance, the leak on our porch, and inexplicable weight gain! I've reached my absolute worry limit!"

"It's just a number," my husband said in a soothing tone. "It doesn't matter. I love you no matter what you weigh."

Sure, sure. Easy for him to say. He's fat, too.

THE BASKETBALL GOAL

I JUST WATCHED MY husband drag the basketball goal from our backyard to the front curb for pick-up. He stood with his hands on his hips and stared down at the battered, rusted rim. I could tell he felt like crying—if men did that sort of thing, of course. The basketball goal on the curb signified the end of an era at our house. No longer would groups of boys stand around in our backyard playing together, drinking Gatorade, challenging one another, and exchanging secrets. They are too old for that now. They've moved on to real gyms, playing pick-up games for exercise, and our years of cheering for our kids from the bleachers have come and gone. My husband is going to miss those days forever. Watching our kids play sports—any game—was his favorite thing to do in the world.

When our boys went to college, it was especially hard on my husband. Since the age of five, our boys played football, basketball, and baseball. Those days were jam-packed. It was always some sports season or another—right through all-star and play-off season in the summer. It made me crazy keeping up with uniforms, carpools, game schedules, concession-stand duty, fundraisers, and all the other jobs parents are assigned when their kids make the team, but my husband reveled in it. He loved every minute of going to games, working the press box or dugout, feeding the team, and interacting with other parents. He fed on it. It was relaxing to him and combined his two favorite things in the world: sports and his kids.

I realized belatedly that his ballpark, gym, and stadium friends were a huge part of his social life, so when our kids grew up, went to college, and no longer played high school sports, my husband's life was impacted in a big way. He grieved over that loss. His job as a presiding appellate court judge is stressful. It's also highly confidential work, so he can't talk to people about it to let off steam. That career would not work for me at all. He doesn't do lunch with the guys very often like I do with my girlfriends, and he rarely talks on the phone, so he felt the loss of those friends much more deeply than I did, especially the folks we were around for many years. In many ways, he lost his community.

I remember when we first put that basketball goal up. It was expensive, more than we could really afford, but my husband was determined to give the boys something they could use all the way through high school. As it turns out, that was a good decision. I overheard lots of brother talk out there from my window upstairs. That was quite helpful, upon occasion.

When I told my oldest son that Dad was taking the goal down, his response was: "My brother never beat me on that goal. I want that on record." His brother's reply: "You cannot believe how much he cheated. It was shocking."

My bet is that someone picks up that goal by the street before lunchtime today. I hope so. I like to think of somebody else's young players giving it a new life. I'm happy to share. If my husband sees it somewhere in the neighborhood, I hope the new owners don't call the police if he stops to watch their kids play and offers them Gatorade and team snacks.

MY FRIEND, SIRI

I GET LOST ALL the time. I'm not talking about being metaphorically lost, either. I mean *lost*. I have no natural sense of direction. I've written about this many, many times. That's because getting lost is a recurring problem for me—like constantly misplacing my reading glasses, ordering French fries even though I know better than that, and giving in to the temptation to order a pizza or Chinese food, which always sounds more appetizing than heating up the leftovers, which would definitely be the smart-money, healthy way to go.

I envy salmon. They are born knowing how to navigate the waters home. Sometimes, they get caught, canned, grilled, or smoked because of their predictability, but I like that, too. Yum. I'm a salmon fan all around. The thought of homeward-bound salmon is pregnant with meaning. I can envision someone turning that into a country song. Even swallows know which direction to fly to return to the same church eaves year after year. Do you know how small bird brains are? There's a reason "bird brain" is an insult. Animals with much tinier brains than I have are doing better than I am with the sense-of-direction deal. I'd give anything to be able to travel effortlessly like the salmon and the swallows. (Do you want to ask me "What kind of swallow?" A Monty Python joke would work well here.)

I've been embarrassed so many times by my poor navigation skills, but I no longer even flinch when friends make fun of me.

"You don't know how to take me home?" a friend once asked me incredulously when I offered her a ride.

"Nope. No clue. You want to turn here or not? It's up to you. I have no opinion," I replied, bold as brass.

Once when my GPS refused to link up with a satellite on a cloudy day, I simply parked in a Target parking lot, pulled out my Kindle, and read for a while until Siri could get a lock on my position. I'm patient like a dog.

GPS is my friend. I have faith in her. I talk lovingly to her when I'm alone in my car. As a writer, I often work speaking events out of town, and I no longer worry that I will be late, unable to find my venue, or too stressed to talk when I arrive. I regularly have no idea what direction I'm going to back out of my own driveway. Every excursion has the potential for exciting detours and unexplored destinations.

It enrages me when my husband climbs in the car with me and argues with the GPS directions. When that melodious, upper-crust British (that's the voice I've chosen) voice interrupts our conversations to say, "Take the second right," it is not uncommon for my husband to begin negotiating with Siri, as if she's seated in the passenger seat beside him getting her kicks out of bossing him around. In his mind, he always knows better. He often answers sarcastically, "I don't think so, Siri. Traffic is going to be backed up this time of day if I take that exit. I know a back way." Of course he does. What a know-it-all.

This behavior lights me up like I'm a Chinese radar control technician, and American fighter pilots have just entered my airspace without permission. I get in a flap.

"Why do you do this?" I ask my husband in exasperation. "Why do you argue with Siri? If you weren't going to follow her directions, why did you ask for them?!" I think he's just showing off when he gets in petty power struggles with Siri. Who does he think he's impressing? Certainly not me!

If you are confident enough to argue with a professional navigation system, then you don't really need the help. Bully for you. I'm happy for you. Pointing out that you know better than Siri, the professional, is just bragging. I don't find bragging attractive. As a person who can't drive across town to a restaurant, I've eaten in a thousand times before without Siri's help, I don't appreciate being taunted. It's bad form and poor sportsmanship. After all, being born with a good sense of direction is just good genetic luck. You didn't do anything to earn it. It doesn't make you smarter than I am. Yelling at me about having a bad sense of direction is like making fun of the boy with terrible acne or a girl with caterpillar eyebrows and beaver-like front teeth.

Those of you who do not need GPS help should leave it for those of us who do. Keep your grubby hands off the "get directions now" Google Maps app on your phone. Put a pin in something else. I have some suggestions for where you could put those pins for those of you who are especially obnoxious. Not everyone appreciates the beauty of GPS. You aren't worthy of the Siri voice of comfort giving you helpful hints in the dead of night as you jump fearlessly on a freeway you've never seen before in your life.

"You don't deserve GPS!" I tell my husband in a snotty voice. He views my passionate declaration as his cue to launch into a longwinded explanation of why the GPS route usually isn't the "best" way, as if this somehow matters to me, which it does not. At all.

I want my GPS to lead the way. That's the whole point of having a GPS. I will follow every strange turn, odd roundabout, and U-turn it suggests. I once allowed it to take me in circles for half an hour before I deviated from the route. I might hesitate if it told me to drive over a cliff or off a bridge. I like to think I would. Everybody makes mistakes. But I'm much more likely to charge down the wrong garden path unaided, so I like my odds following blindly where my GPS leads. GPS may make a mistake now and again, but it has a much higher winning percentage than my dismal on-my-own record. I'll take my chances with the professional.

Following faithfully where my GPS leads is a good pattern for living, too. We should all give up control more often, worry less about every little detour, embrace the twists and turns, and look on each uncharted new mile as an adventure. When is the last time you did that?

MARITAL POTHOLES

---※---

THE HUSBAND OF A long-time friend of mine approached me recently for relationship advice. I love both my friends, so I was anxious to help if I could, even though I'd rather loan them money. That would be less risky. Marital advice is tricky. It often backfires in a big way. The day you urge one spouse to flee the country, confess an affair, hide the credit cards, or forgive an indiscreet kiss will inevitably be a day you rue in the future.

The truth is: down the road, the couple is bound to regret telling you private information about their relationship, and you can't take back the words you say now. It does not matter one bit if every word is true and as good a piece of advice as you've ever given. Some things you just can't say without risking your friendship.

I was sorely tempted. Free advice is the drug of choice for a naturally bossy person like me, and here I was being *asked* for my opinion. How could I resist? Still, this was not my first request for marital advice. The signs ahead said, "Caution," "Turn Back Now— This Means You," "Beware," and "Treacherous Undertow."

My friends recently hit one of the inevitable potholes in the marital road. They're currently stalled out, sunk deep in the mud, completely out of gas, and neither one can see a way to haul themselves out to get back to the journey. They're not sure they are both still headed in the same direction, and even if they are, they are no longer sure they want to continue down the road together.

How's that for an extended metaphor? I could go on all day with that one, I think. A pothole is a deep literary well. Pun intended.

We've been friends for over twenty years, first as young married couples and then later with kids in school together. We tell each other the truth—even when we'd rather not. Mostly, I'd rather not. I'm naturally polite. I began to hope we would be interrupted by an emergency phone call from our kids, an earthquake, or that Jesus would pick this very hour to return for a roll call.

I'm not particularly qualified to give out marital advice. I do have a good friend who counsels for a living, and I offered her up first thing, but that suggestion wasn't greeted with enthusiasm. I think she'd be excellent, I urged, but still no takers. I have no degrees or training, but, as you might guess, I didn't let that stop me in the end.

I once told our beloved pediatrician, Dr. Linda Stone, "One day I'm going to be arrested for practicing medicine without a license. It's practically a requirement of motherhood! I am the arbiter around here of what needs to be stitched or X-rayed and when an illness requires a trip to the emergency room. I could be wrong at any time! I didn't go to school for this!" What I have to offer my friends is a willing ear and a well-stocked bar. Both go a long way when talking through marital trouble, I've found.

I barely had his drink poured before my friend began regurgitating their last argument like a stenographer on steroids. He was startled into silence, his tale of marital woe petering to a halt, when I interrupted to ask what his wife's body language was like during their fight. My friend was visibly confused. He obviously felt like I was wasting valuable fix-it time with irrelevant questions while he was trying to give me the latest report from the battlefield.

I wasn't very interested in the words. I've heard them all before. Like my husband and I, and most people who are in long-term relationships, men and women alike, my friends have the same arguments over and over, with only slight variations. Most of us know our triggers, I think, even if we can't stop the cycle.

I was interested in my friend's body language. It's often more important to pay attention to how people say something than what they say. Was her voice angry or weary? Did she make eye contact? Was she using her hands to punctuate, or were her hands folded in front of her, clenched in fists at her side, or, worst of all, hanging loosely in defeat? Was my friend in a passionate, full-scale rant, or was she merely responding listlessly to whatever he threw out?

An angry partner is not the scariest scenario, I warned him. If she's indifferent or hopeless, it might be more than a pothole. It could be a sinkhole that could suck up the car, both of them, and well-intentioned folks like me standing nearby trying to mind our own business.

Pay attention to the little things, I urged my friend. I've given him this advice at least once a year for over twenty years. If you do, you can repair the sinkhole, drive around it, or abandon the car, grab hands, and run away together.

THE BIG TAN LIE

———————✦———————

ALTHOUGH I LIVE IN the South, I hate hot weather. Yeah. It's unfortunate. "Unfortunate" is such a handy, catch-all word. I know a woman who uses it as her go-to adjective when she can't think of anything good to say. For example, when hearing of someone's ill-mannered grandson whose pyramid scheme bilked thousands of investors at the senior center, her response was "That's unfortunate." "Unfortunate" is almost as good as "You don't say." It covers a multitude of ills. I love a word with vague, hard-to-pin-down connotations. They're very useful in polite social interactions.

For about nine months of the year, it's hot down here. We have many words to describe the various nuances of hot: warm, sultry, steamy, stifling, scorching, hellfire . . . I could go on. I begin dreading the heat and humidity in late spring, and I generally continue to whine until the first cool wave. Sometimes, we have frost on the pumpkins, but just as often I can serve margaritas to the parents of trick-or-treaters. That's just thematically wrong. I like the weather in Great Britain. Bring on the wind and the rain. Those folks start keeling over when the temperature hits the high 80s. Here, there are days when I pray for the high 80s so we can cool off a bit.

To look even marginally attractive, I need a few layers between me and the rest of the world. Sadly, there are only so many layers I can shed in the summer without embarrassing my children or myself. It has come to my attention that somebody needs to point out to the general population that there is a fine line between resort wear and indecent exposure. I volunteer to do that right now.

For those of you who have jumped over the line and straight into attire suitable for the Playboy mansion pool, I urge you to rethink the thong bikini bottoms. Very few people look good in a thong—male or female. There should probably be an age limit for purchasing skimpy bikinis. The law says you have to be twenty-one to buy booze, so maybe we should have a must-be-twenty-one-or-younger statute for itty bitty, teeny tiny, yellow polka dot bikinis—or another color, for that matter. This would be in the best interest of society as a whole. I am the first to admit that no one needs to catch a glimpse under my beach cover-up these days. There are lumps and bumps there I can't even identify, and you can actually count the screws under my skin that hold my knee together after I broke my kneecap on a sheet of ice. Gross.

Apparently, I'm not the only carbohydrate and sugar-eating sinner out there. In truth, most people don't show at their best in summer attire. I went to a church wedding recently in July and spotted a woman in flip-flops. When did beach footwear become acceptable for a wedding? She wasn't recovering from bunion surgery or anything that I could see. She was determined to be comfortable, and she didn't care whose wedding photos she bombed in an effort to keep her own tootsies cool and breezy. This is how low we've sunk.

I have no desire to lie spread-eagle on a beach towel, turning every half hour, baking in the sun like chicken oiled up on a grocery-store rotisserie. First of all, that's boring. Also, I think tanning is melanin-ist. (I initially wanted to say "racist," but that's not my can of worms to open; the struggles of the melanin deficient, however, are all mine.) Think about it for a minute. I was born this color. I may be the whitest person you've ever seen. So what? Why should I be publicly shamed because of my natural skin color? Why should I pay money, spend time, and risk carcinogenic exposure for tanned skin? I'm not a "lay out" on the beach kind of woman. All I do is burn. How is that different from Victorian women applying arsenic powder to their faces? You can't tell me that doesn't sound melanin-ist to you. The truth is obvious. I was born with white skin and dark hair. So be it. I like to think that Snow White's prince would have kissed me right on the lips if he'd seen me first. I'm his type.

All my life, girlfriends, family members, even perfect strangers (particularly snooty sales clerks in boutique clothing stores) have urged me with pinched lips, sardonic eye rolls, and disdainful facial expressions to "get a little sun."

I've never understood the attraction. I get plenty of vitamin D in my daily walks and ordinary, errand-running life. Dermatologists the world over beg patients not to indulge in this senseless self-mutilation, yet many of us continue to worship the sun god like ancient Aztec priestesses. Thousands of people die of skin cancer every year, you know. I just looked up the statistics. They're alarming. And 90 percent of those cancers are due to sun exposure. I've spent years chasing my children around with bottles of sunscreen. Advocating for tanning is like cheerleading for cancer. Like circumcision, body piercings, and tattoos, many of us can't help but bow to the customs of our chosen tribe and kin—even when they're stupid.

In America, particularly, we are socially conditioned to think of tanned skin as healthy, a boon of leisure time spent lolling about on beaches and puttering around in boats. When we see old magazine photo spreads featuring President John Kennedy, his lovely wife, Jackie, and the sandy, sunburned shoulders of their children, Caroline and John, frolicking on sailboats, we don't see sun damage. We see Camelot. But that's what tanning is, of course: evidence of damage—like a roast that browns in the oven. Don't take my word for it. Ask a dermatologist. They have degrees in this! Tanning is a racket. It's a big scam. The whole country is being sold a pig in a poke.

Tanning is big business. Tanning beds, spray tans, over-the-counter lotions and sprays—all are money-makers. In small towns in the South, you can often find a convenience store, a gas station, a fast-food restaurant, and a tanning salon. Not infrequently, all four are housed in the same building for one-stop shopping.

To me, this preoccupation with tanned skin is an oddity, a throwback to a time that makes me feel ill at ease in the here and now. It reminds me of women hobbled for life by feet horribly misshapen after binding them for aesthetic reasons and the legs of furniture that had to be skirted in Victorian times to avoid the scandalous suggestion of bare limbs. Ridiculous! Who makes up these rules? Why in the world would I be tempted to bake and broil the largest organ in my body to change my natural skin color to a more socially acceptable hue arbitrarily deemed "attractive" by current fashion mavens?

Wouldn't we all be happier if we were comfortable living in the skin we were born with—literally and metaphorically? Isn't this what we've all been working toward for so long? I'm a fully grown (in some ways *overgrown*, I'm sad to report) white woman. I'm okay with that, and the rest of the world needs to be okay with it, too.

I'm a native Alabamian. We have a well-documented history of treating people differently based on their skin color. Artificially altering one's skin color, or "passing" as it was called, was once an illegal act. Biologists explain, in much more learned ways than I can here, that racial differences don't actually exist. We are all descended from a few lines. The differences in skin color that make us seem dissimilar, like eye color, hair color, and the like, are merely variations in the line. The differences in race we have historically perceived as real are merely social constructs—like religion, government, or regional patois. Bottom line: my rant about tanning pressure is intended to be humorous social commentary, but the social and historical implications of skin color are no laughing matter.

I can almost see my daughter rolling her eyes and hear her saying, "Ugh, Mom! Lighten up!" as I type this. She's a sun-worshiper, just so you know.

The tanning craze reminds me of another boondoggle: bottled water. Usually, bottled water isn't any healthier than what comes right out of the kitchen tap. When my kids stand at the kitchen sink and twist open a bottle of water I've bought for outings, I want to pull my hair out by the roots. What a waste! I don't see why everyone isn't in agreement with me about this tanning business. I feel like a voice crying in the wilderness when I should hear an "Amen!" from every corner.

When we go on a family vacation, I don't want to pay money to lie on a beach packed with people, their pets, and their music, nor do I want to listen to their fights or smell their cigarette smoke. We have wide, beautiful, white-sand beaches in my home state. Why in the world would I get on a plane and travel thousands of miles and pay big money to arrive at a different beach to do exactly the same thing I can do at home? I want to see places I've never seen before, sample foods I've never eaten, and treat myself to guided tours and museum excursions.

I'm a bus tour fan. I would like to have a tiny, well-informed voice feed a steady stream of information into my ear all the time about the life, people, history, and events playing out in front of me. Wouldn't that be helpful? Feel free to scorn the beach and join me on tour. I'll be the pale-skinned woman in the wide-brimmed hat wearing the 50 SPF sunscreen.

SWEET LIPS

LIPSTICK, IN PARTICULAR, MAKES me feel pretty. I know it's not really a magic potion. My same old dry lips lie underneath the colorful, half-circle smears, but I still believe in the power of lipstick. Oddly enough, I don't have feelings about the rest of my makeup at all, but lipstick is different somehow. Lipstick is the most important item in my makeup drawer. In a pinch, I can make do with only moisturizer and lipstick. This is my standard evacuation beauty plan. It pays to think about such things ahead of time. I live in a volatile weather region. If I have to bug out, rest assured that I will have lipstick tucked in my pocket. These days, I should probably reach for the concealer first, but lipstick has much more power. I'm a Southern woman. I wear red lippy. The sky may be falling, but if I have on a little lipstick, I feel more able to cope with whatever happens next. Lipstick gives me the illusion of control. And, yes, of course I know it's an illusion.

For years, I favored an inexpensive drugstore brand of lipstick, Revlon's Cherries in the Snow, a classic red that's been around since the 1950s. I often blended Cherries in the Snow with other shades to tone it down a bit. Alone, it makes a strong 1950s Hollywood starlet statement. I wrote a whole chapter about this lipstick in a previous book. The manufacturer sent me several lipsticks as a thank-you after the book's release. That is probably the most unusual book thank-you I've ever received. I thought it was a lovely gesture. These days, I've fallen hard for a $38 lipstick by Givenchy called *Framboise Velours*. I just hate that I discovered it because it kills me to pay that much for one lipstick. It's divine. Darn it.

Lipstick reminds me that I'm more than just a mom. I'm a woman, too, even if I'm getting older and fatter every day. You probably shouldn't purse your lips or make fun of me because of my fondness for lipstick. That would be culturally insensitive. The truth is that lipstick is an inexpensive way to buy a little happy in a woman's day. I'm okay with it if men want to buy into our little bit of lipstick happy, too. As far as I'm concerned, there is always room at the makeup counter for a genuine lipstick lover.

During my grandmother's final days in the nursing home, it upset me to see her without lipstick. She wore red lipstick, too. I always dabbed her lips with a little color before I left. I cannot remember her ever wearing anything more than lipstick, powder, and maybe a hint of blush. She was not a product of a cosmetically enhanced generation. The lipstick dabbing at the end of her life was more for me than her; she was beyond such vain concerns. It made me feel better to leave her with that small dignity intact—the smile she always showed the world when she still made her own choices about what to wear and whether or not it was a lipstick-worthy day.

We all have masks that we assume, public personas that we cloak ourselves in like armor to face the trials of our everyday lives. It gives us a sense of control in a world that offers no guarantees of safety, comfort, or happy endings. There's nothing wrong with that. It's natural to want to protect ourselves from anyone who wants to unmask us and see who we are underneath without an express invitation to get up close and personal. I feel sorry for celebrities who can't even dash to the market for milk without applying makeup for fear that an unflattering photograph, with accompanying insulting commentary, speculation, or outright libel, will appear in a grocery store tabloid or online site. Deliberately ambushing people to capture them at their worst is mean.

Lipstick wears off, of course. Nothing superficial lasts. It's the mouth underneath that matters. And that's where we all get in trouble. We have to live with the words that fall from our lips—sweet words of encouragement and praise and also nasty words of malice and discontent. Even a good-hearted person can inflict terrible harm if he or she has an ugly mouth. They don't cancel one another out. Some things can't be unsaid. Once lies, gossip, and other hateful words leave someone's lips, they can't be recalled. They can be forgiven, sure, but they are never really forgotten. It's like a hasty email rant written in the heat of the moment. Once you press send, it's gone. It can't be retracted, and it can be forwarded forever and ever.

I've noticed many times that a smile can transform a face that is lined, old, scarred, or marred, a visage that is distinctly unattractive in the traditional sense, into something breathtakingly lovely. When that happens, it's a beautiful thing to see.

The converse is true, too. A bitter-looking, tightly pursed mouth often reveals a lack of generosity in spirit. You can read a lot about a person by looking closely at his or her face. It's a roadmap of laugh lines, sun wrinkles, and bright, twinkling eyes that often appear youthful, lively, and highly interesting, even when they are almost hidden by the folds of old age.

I know I'm getting a lot of mileage out of this lip metaphor. Sometimes a cigar is just a cigar. Some unlucky individuals simply inherit the gene for skinny lips. It doesn't say anything about their personalities one way or another. I'm generalizing. But I think my theory often holds true. It's not the individual features on someone's face—the symmetry of nose, eyes, or mouth, specifically—that determine whether we see the person as beautiful or not. It's the way that people look out at the world that makes them appear attractive to others. A good heart shines through somehow. A positive attitude seems to shape the whole face, like a light that gets turned on right behind a person's eyes. A bitter person's face can be easily read from across a crowded room. The facial expression is often unnaturally controlled looking. The mouth is tight and unsmiling. Teeth are often clenched. Overall, the viewer's impression is of a person who is guarded, angry, and closed off.

I'm a little worried when I look in the mirror now. My lips aren't particularly plump. I think they're actually thinner than they were just last year. No matter what life holds in store for me in the future, I don't want to end up bitter. I hope to always have a quick smile to offer friends and strangers alike, a generous smile, too, one that is not measured out in careful doses, but rather tossed willy-nilly toward every person who crosses my path.

I COULD DRIVE
A TRUCK

———————✦———————

ONE DAY, I'D LIKE to own a truck. It's true that I've never actually driven a truck, but I feel confident I could handle it. I'm not talking a tractor-trailer or anything with more than four wheels, nor do I want one of those shiny, oversized, souped-up trucks that men purchase in an effort to compensate for . . . whatever. I mean an old-fashioned truck like you see on dirt roads in the country. I often see the trucks I like on the way to the beach. Their drivers meander down the road a tad under the speed limit and hold up traffic. They don't care. There is often a sunburned arm propped on the driver's side window, which is usually rolled down. Just the idea of owning a truck makes me feel useful—like I've just vacuumed the refrigerator coils or found a two-for-one deal on orange juice.

A truck would be handy. Run-of-the-mill trucks are sturdy, practical, and affordable. Those same adjectives could be used to describe me. If I worked as a prostitute, my pimp would probably advertise my services with those exact words. Luckily, I'm not in the market for a career change right now. Laugh all you like, but you never know. I never pass a homeless person without praying thanks be to God that I'm not living there on the side of the road. It could happen, you know. We are all just a few calamities and one terrible addiction away from a very different life. I'm always aware of that.

I'd prefer a nondescript color for my truck—not fire-engine red, no matter how traditional that color choice is. Red trucks are perfect for Matchbox-car play, but it's not what I'm looking to tool around town in. I like that classic blue-green color best, the one that looks like the color people used to paint their porch ceilings in the South. There was a reason our people did that, in case you never heard. It was to fool the birds and keep them from nesting in the eaves. To birds, the ceiling was supposed to look like sky. I guess it must have come as a mighty big surprise to birds that tried to soar through one of those beaded-board porch ceilings. Ouch.

Trucks are useful. Unpretentious. You can haul almost anything in the back of a truck. Logs, a child's playhouse, a canoe, a new washer and dryer, bushels of farmer's market vegetables, or a piano—anything that fits in the truck bed is potential cargo. When I was a kid, it wasn't unusual to see a bunch of kids piled in the back of a pickup, but now that I know how dangerous that is, I could never put a child back there. It sure was fun, though. Bridges and parking decks are the limit with regard to height. It's almost too exciting for me to think about. Just imagine moving house with the aid of a personal truck instead of a rented U-Haul or moving van of professionals. That turns me on like a half hour of foreplay.

I love anything that makes life easier and earns its own keep. You can't ask more of an inanimate object that that. I will happily throw money at a new grill or a laptop computer. Those are sound investments that start giving back to the family as soon as you bring them home. Unfortunately, you can't say that about kids. They suck up time, money, and energy for at least eighteen years before you can expect to see any return on that investment. Also, you can't return kids if you get a lemon, and there are no guarantees they will work properly, perform as intended, or be easy to use. Some assembly is definitely required. I've heard of some kids who seem to be missing pieces when they arrive, and I know kids who occasionally blow up, quit working, or fall apart. There is no guarantee you will get your money's worth, either.

Trucks are versatile. I admire that in a vehicle and a person. I could haul donations for the Bane and Blessing sale at the church or pile enough Christmas greenery in a truck bed to bedeck all my friends' and neighbors' halls with holly. I'd enjoy playing Lady Bountiful with Christmas greenery. I can see myself in that role.

A radio interviewer once asked me to list one adjective to describe myself. The word that popped into my mind was "responsible." I wasn't very happy with that word. I tried to think of another one. It seemed embarrassing. How boring am I if the best way to describe me is "responsible"? I'd much rather be adventurous, brilliant, talented, or beautiful. Surely there's a whole host of better things to be.

The truth is: I am responsible. Like a sturdy, American-made truck, you can count on me. I'm tough, strong, and durable. I weather well. I'm the woman who will help clean up after the party. I'll bring a cake for the funeral luncheon when everyone else flakes out on you. I'll make you soup when you're sick. I'll remember your birthday, eat a cupcake with you even if I'm on a diet, and listen to you when you need to talk about the leak in your bathroom that you can't afford to fix. You can rely on me to be there when you need me. Even if there isn't one thing I can do for you that will actually help, I believe in showing up.

Somehow, that all seems too ordinary to be important, doesn't it? It isn't, though. The more I think about it, the more I realize that just showing up, being available, is a worthy mission in itself. I'm not ashamed of being ordinary. Somebody has to be a worker bee.

I have never cared what kind of vehicle I drive. I want it to start every time I get in it, and I will flat-out leave it on the side of the road if the air-conditioner breaks. That's top-of-the-list important to me. If you live down South like I do, you will understand my hard line there.

I drove a Suburban for seventeen years. The turn signal came on randomly, made a clicking noise, and refused to be turned off by a variety of mechanics who tried for the last seven years I owned it. The door locks quit working in the last three years, so I always had to check all three rows for stowaways before climbing in. It had baseball dents, moldy smells, and gummed-up seatbelt holders. Yet when it came time to sell it, all I could think about was all the things I'd driven my children to in that car. Trading it in seemed like giving up on a faithful friend. I sure don't want anyone to give up on me just because I've got a few years and a lot of miles on me.

Since I drove a Suburban for so many years, I know how it feels to sit high above compact cars. I could roll over a Prius and barely feel the bump in my Suburban. I think I'm ready for a smallish truck. I would be proud to be a truck driver. I saw some Cole Haan loafers just last week that would be perfect driving moccasins.

THE HAIR EXPERIMENT

CONFESSION TIME: I'VE SUNK to a new low. Yesterday, I was a woman whose day—a day I can never get back—was ruined by bad hair. I'm ashamed to admit this to you. It doesn't say anything good about me. It makes me look small and shallow, and I see myself as way more interesting than that. Never in my life did I think I would be this superficial. In fact, I pride myself on being a woman who is above such nonsense. I've been dismissive, contemptuous, and holier-than-thou about women who validate their self-worth based on outward appearances—their clothes, hair, and makeup—all that subjective, oh-so-fleeting beauty.

No matter how many tiaras you collect along the way, physical beauty eventually fades. Aging is inevitable, and it beats the heck out of the alternative—not aging. Death is not a cure-all for aging. When the downhill slide begins, you better have a personality and a brain to fall back on. You can't coast forever on being pretty. Plenty of women (and men) have tried. It never works. In the end, it's just sad.

Apparently, I'm not nearly as evolved as I thought. I tried something new with my hair a few years ago. My stylist promised I'd love it. My hair would be softer, more manageable, and more stylish. She had just learned a new technique, and she was excited to try it out on me. I should have known right then. It's never good to be a test case. It wasn't my first haircut. You'd think I'd know by now not to fall for the latest hair treatment.

I know what looks good on me and what doesn't, and it's unlikely that a new do will be life-changing, much as I might want to believe it could act like fairy dust. The same principle is true for fad diets. There is no magic pill. It all comes down to eating less and exercising more. How dull. No one wants to do that, so we're always searching for the holy grail of diet success.

As you've probably guessed, my hair was not improved by the groundbreaking new salon treatment. In fact, my naturally curly hair looked like I had touched one of those electrostatic balls in a science museum. It was fried. A baby in a stroller stared at me in open-mouthed terror on my way out of the salon. When I opened the door to my house, my cat jumped all the way off the floor in shock and howled in consternation. Instantly, his tail inflated to meet the perceived threat. His tail looked puffy, wide, and bushy— like my hair. He fled under the sofa. Clearly, he could not withstand the vision of beauty I brought in the house.

My husband, a man who always tries to find something positive to say about my appearance, could only stammer out, "What look were you going for?" That was the best line he could come up with. That's when I knew I was in for some hair teasing.

Bad hair was a remarkably humbling experience. I'm not proud of how I handled it. I seriously considered living as a hermit until it had time to grow out. At the time, that seemed like a reasonable response. I was born with good hair, which is lucky since I don't have hair talent. I can't hold a brush and a blow-dryer at the same time. My hair has always fallen in place without too much coercion from me. It's also thick and curly, so even a bad haircut doesn't show up much. Stylists hold me in contempt, but I notice they are quite content to cash checks written by the no-talent client.

I know I shouldn't complain about something as trivial as temporarily fried hair. I do. When I see the bald heads of chemotherapy patients, I realize how silly my hair whining is. The real problem is bigger than bad hair. I am somehow surprised to find myself middle-aged and overweight, and I've discovered, quite unexpectedly, that bad hair is just one more thing I can't bear. It's the final insult. Like many women my age, I often feel invisible, as if I am no longer valuable because I am not young or pretty anymore. I'm a nice person on the inside. I really am. I work hard at it. But I've found that the older I get, the less likely others are to bother finding out about my inside because of my outside.

When did I internalize these meritless values of our youth-worshiping society? Why am I ashamed of my puffy eyes and my grey roots? Why do I spend thousands of dollars attempting to conceal my body's inevitable response to the progression of time? I've always pictured myself as more confident that that. This aging angst is a new thing for me, and, so far, it's not shaping up to be one of my more attractive phases. If one of my friends was making these same observations, I would be quick to tell him or her to suck it up. I would have very little patience for a pity party based on a few wrinkles, fifteen extra pounds, and a failed hair experiment. It feels different when it's me.

I still have a lot to offer. I have wit, wisdom, and decades of experience. I think I'm a better teacher, parent, wife, and friend now than I was when I was young. We waste a lot of talent in our country because of how people look on the outside: age, skin color, gender, fashion sense, presumed sexual orientation, social mannerisms, and regional eccentricities. Let my bad hair be a life lesson for you. You don't want to learn this lesson on your own. There's nothing more wounding than a shot to the pride. It's way more painful than a broken bone. I bet an attack on pride, self-confidence, and personal identity would be a more effective interrogation technique than physical torture. Given a bad hair alternative, I might have picked torture.

T-SHIRT BILLBOARDS

HAVE YOU EVER HAD one of those mornings when no matter what outfit you put on, it simply wasn't the one you wanted to wear? This what-to-wear angst is a frequent problem for me. I often change my outfit several times before heading out the door in the morning. Sometimes, I have costume changes during the day, as well. It takes me forever to pack a suitcase. I always end up overpacking. I need choices. I find it nearly impossible to commit to clothing for future endeavors.

I dress according to my mood. Who knows what kind of mood I'll be in on a trip? I didn't realize this about myself until my daughter educated me one morning when I sailed into the kitchen in khaki pants, a denim shirt, and running shoes.

"Uh-oh," she muttered, so low she counted on me not hearing her passive-aggressive dig, but I'm a mom, so, of course, I hear everything. I also know instinctively when my kids are lying to me, and I have a "witchy thing," as they call it, that lets me know when they are up to no good. These innate gifts have come in handy over the years.

"What?" I asked, mystified as to how I could have already irritated my daughter so early in the morning without opening my mouth.

"You're in a mood," she said.

"I most certainly am not! Why would you say such a thing?" I demanded, indignant.

"You have on work clothes. You only dress like that when you want to accomplish something. You drag the whole family into your projects like you're a black hole sucking the joy out of the universe. You want us to clean out something, don't you?" she moaned bleakly, laying her head on the kitchen counter in an overly dramatic fashion, as if the world were about to come to an end, and she hadn't had time to straighten her hair.

"Sit up," I demanded without even thinking. "You're getting pancake syrup in your hair."

I gave my daughter's theory that I dressed according to my mood some thought. Could she be right? Most often, I wear black, grey, or white. I wonder what that says about me? Probably nothing good. Occasionally, I add a dab of blue green because that's my favorite color. Most days, I wear black leggings and whatever big shirt or jacket covers up all my sins. I dress primarily for comfort, but I'm vain enough to want to look pretty, too, at least on some level. I have no desire to look like someone living on the streets. I have standards. I don't aspire to win any beauty contests, but I don't want to embarrass my family either. My goal is to blend in. I don't want to stand out by wearing anything too outrageous, inappropriate, or trendy.

Most important, I think, is the fact that I'm always clean. I shower every morning and read in a bubble bath every night. Honestly, I don't think my daughter has anything to complain about. I could look way worse. I still make an effort, for goodness sake, unlike some of my friends who have taken to wearing black exercise pants everywhere. Some of them don't even exercise. Ever. You can't do that if you want to live long enough to qualify for a senior citizen discount at the movies. I'm looking forward to that.

I'm not twenty. I can't scrape my hair up in a high ponytail, throw on shorts and a T-shirt, and still look good enough to photograph for a magazine simply because I'm young, have perfect skin, fabulous hair, expensively straightened teeth, and a rockin' body. Those days are long gone. Truth be told, I never looked as good as my daughter, even when I was her age. She's really pretty, and I don't say that just because I love her. Empirically speaking, she's attractive. If I had any doubts about that, they have been cleared up when I accompany her anywhere. Boys in her vicinity stop talking. Sometimes, they just start following in her wake. I, on the other hand, am rendered invisible. She rarely notices her entourage, I'm pleased to report, but I've sent a few boys scampering once or twice with a big-mama stare.

I don't expect to look like a young girl. I'm over that disappointment, which is a good thing since there is no turning back the clock. These days, I'm well read, have good health insurance, an excellent credit rating, and a wicked sense of humor. My daughter is lucky. She could have a stupid mother who borrows her clothes, pierces an eyebrow, or attends her school functions drunk as a skunk and wearing a tube top and a micro-mini skirt. She really should count her blessings.

I recognize that clothing is more than a nod to modesty or a colorful means of keeping out the cold. It makes a statement. Culture. Age. Income. Personality. Some people feel free to share their most intimate thoughts on T-shirts. I find that shocking. I would never do that. I recently stopped dead in the street when I passed a young man wearing a T-shirt—right out in public for the entire world to see—which said, "Happiness is a _____." Let's just say it was explicitly sexual and leave it at that. I'm not prudish at all, and still that T-shirt knocked the breath out of me. I didn't need to buy a vowel. I could fill in the blanks myself, and I wanted to wash that boy's mouth out with soap and make him turn that shirt inside out.

I admit to some fashion faux pas in my day. The fashion industry has occasionally sucked me in just like everyone else. I challenge you to find one fully grown woman who believes low-riding jeans were a good idea. You won't be able to do it. Low-riding jeans were marketed with classic bait-and-switch salesmanship. We see tall, thin, willowy models wearing new fashions that look wonderful on them, so we think they will look attractive on the rest of us. What we fail to remember is that those models would look equally good in anything—pillowcases, even. It's easy to be fooled. The fashion industry is loaded with talented con artists.

Increasingly, there seem to be outfits for every human activity. Even our hobbies require themed attire these days. God forbid that you jump on a bike in regular clothes. Cyclists are heavy into theme attire. I think they look silly. When I pass them in my car, I often snicker to myself. I think I'd rather be fat than wear those clothes to exercise.

Now that I've taken the time to consider, perhaps I need to put a little more thought into the statements I make to the world every morning with my clothing selection. Who knows what I've been saying about politics or religion with my daily fashion choices? It's possible I've been culturally insensitive. I need to give this further reflection. I need to read the "made in" labels. I'm a proud American. And there are lots of banned dyes now, aren't there? I should pay attention to that. And child labor laws aren't exactly universal, are they? These days, even a morning run has become fraught with potential political disaster.

PERCHANCE TO DREAM

——————✦——————

CHRONIC SLEEP DEPRIVATION IS one of the most common complaints in America. It's certainly one of my biggest trials. Apparently, it makes us all grumpy and fat. That's not just my opinion, either. There are well-educated researchers who probably used my tax dollars to prove it. You can go online and read their reports, or you can just take my word for it. Have I ever lied to you? Remember: I write creative nonfiction.

A good night's sleep is so rare for me that when I wake up naturally, without an alarm, after having slept soundly for eight hours or so, I feel almost drunk, giddy, and uncharacteristically happy and pleased with my lot in life. This is such an unusual frame of mind for me that it makes my children nervous.

"What's wrong with you today?" my son queries.

"I got plenty of sleep!" I respond gleefully.

"Settle down," my son says. "You're being weird."

A surfeit of sleep makes me want to plan a party, clean out the basement, or try out a new recipe for Thai food.

If we could find a way to bottle the natural high we get from a good night's sleep, we could live off our commission checks for the rest of our days. Sleep is the no-cost fix for depression, anxiety, ADD, weight loss, wrinkles, and could significantly decrease the number of on-the-job accidents. I'm telling you: sleep is the solution to all our problems. Now, if we can just get eight hours every night—no matter where we sleep, with whom we sleep, and what is on our minds—we'd be in racing form every day.

Sleep makes me feel invincible. I am a warrior princess, a domestic machine, a writing whirlwind, and an aging sex goddess. Tax season? Bring on Uncle Sam! I can figure it out! Peace summit among African war lords? I'm telling you: If I have eight hours of uninterrupted sleep, I can broker a deal.

Sleep is the key to optimism. If I were in charge of the troops, I'd hand out those "go" and "no-go" pills they have in their packs like breath mints. I'd want my team fighting fit, and a decent night's sleep would be a good place to start. Soldiers regularly have their fingers on the trigger of automatic weapons. It's a no-brainer to me that they need their beauty rest. I want them clearheaded and ready to rock when they're guarding my embassies. Bad guys are sneaky, and they probably just lie around all the time sleeping before going on the attack. I want our military boys and girls in tip-top shape.

I've never been a good sleeper. I can't turn my brain off. It runs on a continuous hamster wheel of worries about children, work, family, friends, and the fate of the world in general. I wake up easily, at the slightest sound or movement, and then I can't go back to sleep. I move from room to room with a book and a book light and check repeatedly that all my children are asleep in their beds. I look like a menopausal tooth fairy trying to round up some business from an older crowd.

As a young mother, I was sleep-deprived because I had to be awake at all hours of the night feeding, changing, comforting, and nursing my kids. Now the same kids have turned me into a clock-watching curfew zombie. I worry about whether my kids are wearing their seatbelts or not and if they've been drinking or riding with someone who has been drinking. Teenagers are not known for their smart decision-making. Their frontal lobes aren't fully developed. It's simple biology. We operate under the Reagan doctrine in this house: trust but verify.

I'm a worrier. Worriers do not sleep well. I wish I could change this about myself, but I don't know how. I've tried everything:

relaxation techniques, warm baths, herbal teas, drugs, and turning off the television and computer screens early. Nothing works for me. I seem fated to be one of those people who tosses and turns in bed listening to others snore. Even my cat snores. He sleeps at least twenty-two hours a day. It amazes me. I'm jealous. I'd be willing to stretch out underneath the dining table, too, if catching a sunbeam would work for me. I'm not too proud for that.

The truth is: I sleep well when I'm happy. That means all my kids are home, and none of them are mad at me. My husband and I have to be getting along well. My work can't be too stressy, and I have to have a realistic plan to pay my credit card bill. My close friends' and family members' lives have to be in good shape, too. Also, I can't sleep if I've watched one of those heartbreaking commercials from the Salvation Army or the Humane Society right before bed. They make my stomach hurt and my eyes tear up.

A good night's sleep is a high bar for me. How often does the perfect-sleep storm happen in your life? Almost never, right? It's the stuff of dreams. That's right. My sleep fantasy is . . . sleep.

EAU DE BOY NEEDS

IT'S DIFFICULT, SOMETIMES, FOR me to distinguish my wants from my needs. I am like a child who says, "Mommy, I need a cookie!" "No, you want a cookie," I remember correcting my own child. After considering for a second, my son said, "No, Mommy, I *need* a cookie!" He got what I meant; he just disagreed with my definition of need.

In reality, of course, my needs, like everyone's, are simple: food, shelter, companionship . . . and maybe the occasional antibiotic. The problem is that I think I need a number of other things to be happy. By definition, they are not needs. They are wants.

For example, I think I need bubble baths, chocolate, books, and the occasional pair of fabulous shoes. The blurry lines between wants and needs get us all in trouble. We are a nation of credit card debtors. We want what we want when we want it. Saving up for something is considered old-fashioned. We have so many luxuries that they are no longer categorized as luxuries. We're spoiled. I'm as guilty of this as anyone, no question about it.

My favorite luxuries—things I consider needs and not wants—are ice, hot water, and air-conditioning. I like my creature comforts. I have been known to call my husband and threaten to charge a car on my credit card if the air conditioning goes out again, and I sometimes avoid restaurants because "they don't have good ice." (I can't believe how much I'm telling on myself in this book. It's a litany of my sins. Go ahead. Let my life serve as a cautionary tale for you. I will not have lived in vain.)

Because of my frequent inability (or unwillingness) to make fine distinctions between my wants and needs, I sometimes make poor choices about how to spend money. In a department store dressing room, I often think that I need to buy a new outfit. I justify my splurge by saying it will make me look pretty, confident, and nicely camouflaged. Later, when I balance my checkbook and realize there are more important bills I need to pay instead, I'm invariably remorseful. The line between my needs and wants comes instantly into focus like the main feature right after the blurry previews are over in a movie theater.

When gazing at my rear end in a three-way department store mirror, I honestly believe that black pants that make me look fifteen pounds lighter are worth any price. I'm willing to sell a kidney on the black market to take those suckers home with me.

This bad behavior on my part reminds of one of my favorite Flannery O'Conner short stories, "A Good Man Is Hard to Find." The grandmother in the story has her needs and wants clarified for her instantly when she is held at gunpoint. I, too, would be a good woman if there were "someone there to shoot [me]" every minute of my life.

Although I think a gun would be an effective means of making me put down the black pants, I'm searching for a less drastic way to keep myself in line. Surely, there is something better.

I'm good in a crisis. I can triage, adapt on the fly, and run through even limited choices quickly. I'm calm in an emergency, and I make good decisions under pressure. Blood doesn't faze me. I get tunnel vision in life-and-death situations. Believe it or not, I probably make better decisions then than I do with the little, everyday decisions in life—like whether or not I should buy black pants I can't really afford.

There is nothing like the threat of death, calamity, or the end of days to focus our minds on what is really important. That's how cult leaders prey on ordinary people. They tap into people's needs and wants, blur the lines, and use fear to convince followers to drink the

Kool-Aid. Waiting on the results of a risky surgery, worrying about whether or not a son or daughter passed an important exam, or hoping against all logical expectation for a rescue from a rooftop during a natural disaster—these are the life-changing moments when our needs and wants separate themselves easily into tidy mental boxes. But these aren't the trials of everyday life, and we quickly forget how easy it was to categorize our needs and wants when life returns to "normal."

When I picked up my son after a two-week session at summer camp one July, I unpacked his trunk outside on the front porch so I could sort the dirty clothes, shoes, trash, and assorted detritus boys accumulate at summer camp. I always take three garbage bags with me for porch sorting: one for garbage, another for clothes that might be salvaged by multiple washings and a cup of bleach, and a third for wet, mildewed clothes and towels. I'm a seasoned hand. You'd be amazed by how much sand, candy wrappers, leaves, and sticks— even a few bugs, living and dead—boys bring home with them in their camp trunks.

I suspect it takes them approximately two minutes to pack their gear for the return home. They just walk around their cabins, collect stuff that might or might not belong to them, throw it all in the trunk, and sit on the lid to force it to close. If you've never unpacked for a hot, sweaty, stinky boy in summer, you can't appreciate the aroma of eau de boy. I gagged many, many times over the years.

Imagine my shock when I opened the trunk (taking care to stand a few feet back from the initial wave of smell) to begin the annual sorting and discovered the contents of my son's trunk were in pristine condition. The beach towel I'd carefully rolled around sunscreen and his swimsuit, his shorts, shirts, and socks—they were all carefully folded, just as I'd packed them originally. Nothing in the trunk had been disturbed. At all. For two weeks.

When I called my son outside to question him about this mystery, he shrugged and said he hadn't needed anything.

"Didn't you go swimming?" I asked, incredulous.

"Sure. I swam in my shorts," he replied. "They dried."

"Did you take a shower?" I demanded.

"No need," he said. "I told you we swam EVERY DAY."

Needs and wants—sometimes I need a reminder. I bet you do, too.

I WISH I LIVED HERE

WHEN I ASK FOR forgiveness from someone, it's the things I've left undone, sins of omission, that bother me most—not the sins of commission. I'm in fairly good shape with the commandments. Although I've threatened it upon occasion, I've never actually killed anyone. Yet. I admit that I've been tempted. Who hasn't? The point is: I didn't actually commit the crime. I haven't been adulterous. Jealousy isn't one of my sins, and I'm quite fond of my parents. I find them easy to honor. What I aspire to do well, but often fall short on, are the "should have," "would have," and "could have" items that I never seem to get around to, despite my good intentions. I fear my epitaph will say, "Here lies Mel. She meant well."

Like almost every mom I know, I feel like I hurtle through my day at a breakneck pace, like Miss Clavel, the nun in the illustrations for the *Madeline* books. School, work, cook, clean, laundry, sleep and then begin all over again! Hurry, hurry!

Most days, I field whatever ball comes my way, put out the closest fire, and tread water just hard enough to keep from going under. This is no way to live! I call the parenting I've done with three offspring close in age "triage parenting." I'm just trying to get the big things right. Work hard. Plan ahead. Do your part. Help those less fortunate than you are. Forget the old stop-and-smell-the-roses cliché! I'm lucky if I notice I have flowers blooming in my yard at all. Usually, I toss out a few annuals every year and hope for the best. If birds can get wildflowers to sprout—and they do—with their unintentional, inelegant manner of seed distribution, I don't see why I can't do at least as well, but that's a saga for another essay.

Just thinking about my to-do list makes me tired before I even get out of bed. When I look around my house, all I see is the dust so thick you could write your name in it on the dining table, the piles of laundry yet to be sorted, and the crusty pots and pans that wouldn't fit in the dishwasher no matter how much I rearranged the dishes the night before. The sad truth is that I'm too concerned about the things that don't matter in the long run to take stock of the things that matter right now. Even though I know this about myself, I continue to make this mistake over and over again. I don't know why I can't internalize this lesson once and for all.

Over the years, each one of my three children has invited a child into our home who looked around and uttered some variation of these words: "I wish I lived here." They could have said "I wish my mom made after-school snacks," or "I wish my parents helped with homework," or "I wish I could count on my dad to pick me up on time."

They didn't.

When a child says these words to you and means them, you know it in your heart immediately. Each time it happened to me, I looked around my house and saw it with new eyes. It was the same old house—leaky gutters, outdated bathrooms, chipped kitchen counters, carpet stains, cat hair everywhere, and handprints on the walls. But my eyes saw the view from a new perspective—through the eyes of a child who longed to live here with us. Over and over again, I need this lesson reinforced. I take my ordinary, everyday-kind-of-wonderful life for granted. I've got to quit doing that.

ONE GOOD THING

HAVE YOU EVER HAD one of those weeks that was so overwhelming to you, undermining to your self-confidence, and discouraging to your heart that you became weirdly focused on getting one small thing right, as if that one act alone could salvage the entire week? This week, nothing went well for me. I could not catch a break.

One of my students stopped coming to class, and I haven't been able to find the carrot or stick to lure him back. I will eventually. Trust me. I don't give up easily.

On another front, I inexplicably gained five pounds, and I didn't even cheat on my diet. Much. That was depressing, too.

One of my kids has decided he wants to be a poet and street musician. He thinks a graduate degree in creative writing sounds like a lot more fun than finishing law school. Well, who doesn't think that? I would love to take classes in any old subject that interests me: Plato, Egyptology, vampire literature, and genetics. I like books about those subjects. That doesn't mean I get to do that! I need a paycheck and health insurance, and so does my son.

Writing deadlines loom on my horizon, but, sadly, I have nothing to write about right now. My brain feels sluggish and dull. That's unusual. I almost always have an opinion about any subject. The legal fight to give apes fundamental rights to life like people have—as opposed to being considered legal things—interests me, for example. This is a real debate. I'm not making it up. I watched a TED Talk about it last night. I don't handle writer's block well. I'm not accustomed to it.

One cure for a crummy week, when nothing in my personal or professional life is going well, is to find a small task that I can accomplish, feel good about, and gain absolute dominion over. To get to this feel-good-about-oneself satisfaction, some people drink, have sex, shop with a vengeance, or go on food binges. I've tried those, but nothing makes me feel better than accomplishing something—no matter how small.

Today I woke up with a mission. I'm not going to cure cancer or balance my checkbook or anything Herculean like that. I'm a reasonable person looking for a little on-the-job satisfaction to make me feel better about myself. I need something good to come out of this week. I need a tangible, calculable, visible success story which will give my life meaning. My mission: to teach myself to fold a king-sized fitted sheet so that it will fit neatly on my linen closet shelf.

I know it sounds impossible. I've tried and failed to scale this mountain many times over the years, but I have newfound insight and up-to-date research. This time will be different because I have watched YouTube videos featuring pretentious domestic know-it-alls who make this task look easy. Martha Stewart demonstrated a technique for success that seemed attainable to amateurs like me. She didn't even muss her hair folding that sheet. I always end up wrestling with it like I'm trying to rope a calf at a rodeo. I end up using my arms, legs, feet, and even my mouth and chin.

The messy mound of sheets in my closet is one of the small irritants in my life. When I open the linen closet on sheet-changing day, I do so with bated breath and extended arms. There is always the danger of sheets raining down on my head from the top shelves.

I've tried everything to sort that disaster. I stuck labels on the shelves. I put matching sheet sets in pillowcases so sheet-changers in this family could reach in and grab a pillowcase without rummaging through stacks and messing everything up like squirrels hiding their nuts for winter.

I tried separating flat and fitted sheets and, alternately, matching coordinating sheet sets like socks. That worked for a while, but it didn't last. I deeply regret buying plain-colored sheets when I married; they are indistinguishable from one another. I should have bought brightly colored patterned sheet sets that are easy to differentiate, even if they caused my kids to have epileptic seizures in their sleep.

After watching Martha painstakingly fold a fitted sheet into a perfect square, I tried my best to imitate her work. Over and over. For fifty minutes. Eventually, I muted her voice on my laptop. I'm pretty sure she was taunting me, personally, in the video. No matter how hard I tried, I simply could not do it. It reminded me of the day I tried to clean our icemaker. I had the instructions laid out on the kitchen counter. There were pictures. No matter how hard I tried, I could not match up the pictures with the corresponding parts in the icemaker. It felt like the illustrator for the instruction pamphlet was deliberately leading me astray. It could have been written in Farsi for all the good it did me.

It would undoubtedly be easier for me to learn how to perform an appendectomy than to master the art of sheet folding. Even if I get the folds to look right, they don't stay. When I open the linen closet, my perfectly folded sheets still spring to life like an old-fashioned Jack-in-the-box.

Nothing (even sheet-folding) worked for me this week. The point is: I'm not giving up. No matter what. I'm going with Winston's "Nevah, nevah, nevah give in" advice. I saw some baskets at the dollar store that might be the perfect solution. I'm optimistic about finding a better way to attack this high-thread-count problem. No matter what, I always remind myself, *Next week is just around the corner.* Sometimes, you have to will yourself to be optimistic. You don't have to feel it. You just have to fake it. I tell my children the same thing about good manners. Good manners aren't always heartfelt. We've all faked it to get through some awkward moments. It's our social contract. We've all agreed to play along and keep the faith. Some weeks, that's the best we can do.

STAINED GLASS
WINDOWS

---◆---

I THINK STAINED GLASS windows are one of the ways we humans rise above our earthly confines to prove that we are, as unlikely as it seems, fashioned in the image of God. How do you like those big words? I'm holding nothing back with this book. It must be turning fifty. I'm filtering less and less. I'm calling the game of life like I see it and telling you straight up what I believe and why that should interest you, too.

Writing small—but fiercely important, in my opinion—observations about the world is my job. I think it's a writer's responsibility to use our chosen tools, words, to describe, observe, comment upon, and generally provide helpful translation for readers all over the world. Here I just happen to be writing about stained glass windows.

I've come to realize that people are not as far apart in thinking as we've been led to believe by those who would exploit those divisions for their own ends. We just use different vocabularies based on where and when we were born, what gender we identify with, what social group we represent, how educated or uneducated we are, and what formative experiences have shaped us.

Humans never cease to surprise me. I mean that in glorious ways and also horrifying ones. We gun each other down in silly squabbles and reveal depths of depravity that are hard to comprehend. But we also use our abilities to create works of art for the sheer joy of it. I am in awe of talent like that: painters, sculptures, and, yes, even stained-glass-window makers—people who create such beauty with their own hands that I look upon them and forget how to breathe for a few minutes.

Stained glass windows are my favorite art form. I like everything about them: the variety of size and scale, the rich colors, the intricate scenes or patterns depicted in them, the unique vision brought to life by each artist's interpretation, the historical connections to buildings that house the windows, and even the dedications and "in memory" plaques that often accompany them.

Historically speaking, the materials, dedicated time, and skilled craftsmanship necessary to create such works of art were financed by sponsors who were then rewarded for their support with the boon of a dedication. Sometimes, sponsors are allowed to choose the scene, which the artist then renders in his or her own style. Art patronage and the purchase of religious indulgences are ancient customs. The stories surrounding the creation of works of art, like famous stained glass windows, would be good inspiration for a series on the History Channel. I'd watch that. Would you?

I am always happy to deviate from any trip I take to view exceptionally crafted stained glass, despite the long-suffering sighs and frustrated eye rolls from my children or husband. If the window is enclosed in the walls of an ancient chapel or cathedral, that's even better, as far as I'm concerned. I'd like to tour the building, too. I'm convinced that these windows are the closest I will ever come to a view of heaven from this side of the pearly gates. It may be as close as I ever get. I'm not exactly saint material. I can't afford to miss out on a single one while I'm still alive, willing, and able to climb through brambles to get a closer look.

I have a friend, Morgan Murphy, who created, with his own hands, the stained glass windows in his kitchen. He took a class to learn how, which did not surprise me one bit. He's a twenty-first-century, bigger-than-life figure, a nimble thinker with a wicked sense of humor and more talents than I can count. His kitchen windows have jokes (in Latin, no less) embedded in the brilliantly hued bits of glass and lead.

They illustrate sayings like "If you can't stand the heat, get out of the kitchen!" Don't you just love that? When I first saw them and sucked in an awed breath, he was pleased that I got the joke. Nobody reads Latin anymore. I think that's a shame for a bunch of reasons.

It seems unlikely that I could write anything new or profound to describe the light that flickers through stained glass windows. I'm sure the greeting card industry has covered all the bases with regard to the adjectives that immediately spring to mind, but because it is one of my favorite views, I feel compelled to use my own words to interpret the visual for you. I'm a writer. We always think we can write about any subject a little bit better than anybody else.

When the light streams through the ruby-red robes of Jesus, the lapis blue of Mary's cloak, the dazzling white of a lamb, or the golden wings of seraphim immortalized for generations in stained glass, it is almost too much for my eyes to absorb. I can only focus on one aspect of the scene at a time. Apparently, that's not just me. This is literally true for all of us. I read recently about how our vision works, and the brain only allows us to see bits and pieces of any scene. We don't take in a whole scene at one glance, even though we think we do. There are some interesting social experiments studying this if you want to read more about it. I found it surprising.

The view of a magnificent stained glass window is, I think, the physical embodiment of hope. That's the best way I can describe what I see when I view them.

Of course, the light has to be just right. In fact, you need multiple viewings of a stained glass window, at different times of the day and night, to fully appreciate all it has to offer. And one has to stand in the perfect spot to get the full effect—not too close and not too far away. When all the variables are aligned perfectly, light pours through the colored glass like the hand of God has directed it just for the viewer's benefit at that specific moment in time. It makes me feel hopeful about how the human story will turn out. So much talent and beauty—it may ultimately be our saving grace.

THE HOUSECLEANING HARRIDAN

I DESPISE HOUSECLEANING. UNFORTUNATELY, I love a clean house. Therein lies the problem. Since for most of my life there was absolutely no wiggle room in my housekeeping budget (or any other way to fudge it that I could figure out with my poor math skills) to pay professionals to clean for me, I had to suck it up and clean my smelly, sticky, dirty house myself. This is an old song for me, so if you've heard me rant about this before, feel free to sing along.

Five people live in this house. Oddly enough, I seem to be the only neat freak. That's *unfortunate*. While I see cleaning as a weekly necessity—like maintaining a big enough toilet-paper stash to withstand a modern siege, putting away Christmas decorations as soon as the twelve days of Christmas are over, waxing my upper lip so I don't look like a Greek fisherman, and hoarding chocolate bars in my sock drawer for emergencies—not everyone in my family values living in a clean house as much as I do. They are happy with a clean*ish* house. Just so you know: there is a lot of distance between clean and clean*ish*.

I feel short of breath when I see sweating drink glasses—nary a coaster in sight, even though I've scattered them in every conceivable location like Easter eggs before a hunt—placed carelessly on antique wooden tables throughout my house. Every morning, I round the rooms in my house collecting discarded glasses as if I'm off to the glass recycling plant to collect money to feed my starving children.

I am far too persnickety to shower in a bathroom with enough hair littering the floor to make wigs. It is unfathomable to me how every person in my house can simply ignore the presence of human hair in inappropriate places. In my opinion, a wad of hair calls for immediate cleanup—and, upon occasion, a team of crime scene investigators.

I cannot prepare breakfast on kitchen counters with crumbs on them from midnight snacks, and I am not amused when my sneakers make sucking sounds as I stumble across a sticky floor. Filth lights me up, and when I reach the limit of all the mess I can tolerate, heads have been known to roll.

I've tried all the tricks. I'm only one-fifth of the household. Why should I do all the cleaning? Yep. You've read between the lines there. How perceptive of you. I'm a tad resentful. If everyone pitched in, it wouldn't be such a backbreaking task every cleaning day! In fact, if everyone had the decency to tidy up after himself or herself, the big jobs would be easy-peasy.

Prepare yourself. I'm getting warmed up. I feel an urge to find a hot microphone, some banner paper, and a big Sharpie to create a sign-up sheet for a free-the-house-cleaner march on . . . well . . . I can't think where we'd march to. Nobody cares about us tidy folk.

I've tried divvying up cleaning jobs among everyone who lives here. In fact, there are a few kids who don't live here, technically, but who are here often enough they should have jobs, too. I've conscripted volunteers in my house like a warlord on a rampage through suburbia.

I've begged, screamed, cried, threatened, and bribed. I once dabbled in a whiteboard, master-list plan with a built-in incentive system, check boxes, and candy rewards. It took me half a day to make the poster. It was very colorful. It all came to naught. Nagging the rest of my household to do their jobs was more work than doing them myself, so I gave up. What can I say? I'm old, tired, and cranky.

I play games with myself, too. Instead of spending one full day cleaning every week, which is miserable and impossible to schedule on a regular basis, for a few years, I divided the cleaning into five days, about an hour each day. This works as well as anything else I've tried. Bonus: I gave myself the weekends off because I think I'm a stellar employee. Also, I don't hold myself to very high standards. We all make compromises. I can live with this level of clean.

Housecleaning is like exercise. I don't enjoy either one, but I'd prefer not to die of a preventable heart attack or a new strain of mold, so I attend to them. When my kids complain about unpleasant aspects of their part-time summer jobs, I remind them: "I don't like MOST of my jobs! That's life! Everything isn't fun!" When these words come out of my mouth, my kids look at me as if I'm making this truism up just to get on their nerves.

One day, my kids will be forced to clean their own homes before the city condemns them as a community health hazard. That could happen. That would be so embarrassing! They don't publish those condemnations in the paper, do they? I guess it won't really matter; nobody reads the newspaper anymore. There are so few dailies. That little tragedy is a matter we should discuss later.

You better believe I'll make sure I've had all my shots before visiting houses my kids clean. I love my children, but I wouldn't take a shower in their bathrooms for all the tea in China until I cleaned them myself. With bleach.

THE APPLIANCE GODS

---❖---

APPLIANCE GODS ARE REAL. No voodoo ritual, Old-Testament-style sacrifice, or cast-out-the-demon rite will rid your home of this pagan infestation. If nuclear war breaks out, only roaches, telemarketers, political pollsters, and appliance gremlins will be left unscathed. These are mean-spirited, petty, conniving, nasty sprites that live in ventilation ducts, refrigerator coils, and septic tanks. Nothing pleases them more than sabotaging top-of-the-line appliance purchases the day after the warranty expires. They are jealous, spiteful gods who didn't get enough attention from their water heater mamas. We all pay the price for dysfunctional appliance families.

Currently, my dryer sounds like we've tossed a load of scrap metal in with the pool towels to dry. Technically, the dryer still works, so my husband covers his ears and sings la-la-la when I lobby for a new one. It will never be said that we gave up on an appliance in our house too soon. I feel the VISA charge looming. I'm preparing myself.

The unexpected appliance deaths are what I find soul crushing. Just when I save up enough money to repair my dangerously crumbling driveway or treat myself to new (alas, even bigger) fat jeans, an appliance in our house explodes, leaks, overheats, or threatens to electrocute the next person who touches it.

I am accustomed to living with household eccentricities. My house is almost 100 years old. Everything is a little bit special. The dishwasher refuses to fill unless you turn it on and off twice, jump up and down, and ask nicely. Only three of four slots in our toaster pop up, and strips of classy silver duct tape hold the condiments in our refrigerator door, which also fails to latch unless I add a hip check to prove I mean business.

I'm willing to cut some slack for appliances that have served faithfully through three presidential administrations, but I draw the line at fear of electrocution. That's too much. For a few months, my children refused to turn off the chandelier in the living room because it occasionally zapped them with enough voltage to singe the hair on their arms.

"You want to risk it, go ahead," my son muttered one night as he slid through the door at curfew. "I'm young. I have a long life ahead of me. I'm not touching it again until you call a real electrician. This is above Dad's pay grade."

I called the man. Of course I called the man. I'm not unreasonable.

When our water heater dumped fifty gallons of water in our basement, it was 6:15 p.m. on a Friday. A call to a plumber on golden time meant he could send his kid to college on us—a private, Ivy League college. My daughter and I were alone when Niagara Falls began cascading into our basement. We searched frantically for a cut-off valve as water splashed our ankles. Eventually, we spotted a water main inside a creepy crawl space.

"I'm not reaching in there!" I shouted over the sound of rushing water. "No telling what's in there!"

"You have to!" my daughter screamed back at me. "You're the mom! It's your job! I'm just a kid!"

I knew I should have read that job description more carefully. Every day it's something new. Vomit, dog poop in sneaker crevices, and now indoor flooding on a gather-the-animals-two-by-two scale.

No matter how many sacrifices we drag to the street or haul to the dump to appease the appliance gods' sensibilities, it's never enough. They lie in wait—plotting coups, coordinating strikes, and inciting appliance rebellions from the laundry room. When they see an opportunity to cause extreme inconvenience, unexpected expense, or marital squabbles, they attack.

Since the advent of organized, monotheistic religion, the appliance gods have been relegated to dust-bunny obscurity. They're unhappy, a little bored, and aggrieved. It's best not to underestimate them.

THE CHRISTMAS
GREENERY THIEF

FIRST OF ALL, I want to remind you that I write nonfiction. Sure, I exaggerate upon occasion. I'm a Southerner. Hyperbole is my friend. I know how to tell a story and make it worth listening to, but in the following incident, I didn't make up one word. I swear. I didn't have to. As so often happens, real life is colorful enough down here where I live. Here's the play-by-play:

It was the day reserved for the holiday greenery sale to the public at the botanical gardens in the city where I live. When I arrived, the usual hustle and bustle was in full swing. Women all over the place were talking to themselves as they considered how much greenery was needed in each room of their houses and porch spaces. In no time, my arms were too full to see over my foliage, so I placed my selections in a pile and began scoping out the rest of the aisle for anything I might have missed to bedeck my halls. I was proud of my haul. I came early on purpose, and it paid off. I had some primo specimens, and everything smelled wintery and fragrant.

Imagine how shocked I was when a fellow shopper blew right by me and whisked my pile of bodacious greenery into her arms without even making eye contact or acknowledging me standing there in my garden clogs. She headed for the checkout counter at a gallop, leaving me immobilized in her wake with my mouth hanging open like a low-IQ mouth breather. The truth is: I was too surprised to react. My clogs were frozen in place right next to a pile of parasitic mistletoe someone had been brave enough to climb a tree to collect for shoppers like me who remain hopeful, even after all these years, that someone, somewhere, some day will feel compelled to lay a big kiss right on our lips if we continue to tack it over every available doorway. Hope springs eternal in a woman's breast, no matter how old or saggy the breast is. This is an evergreen truth.

"I'm so sorry," I called out to the greenery thief, trying to get her attention.

(I'm a Southern woman, and we often begin our sentences with "I'm sorry," whether we're taking responsibility for monsoon rains a continent away or starving children in North Korea. We're trained to take the blame from an early age, to please as many people as possible, and to apologize to those we can't, no matter how impossible they are to please.)

"I think you've mistakenly nabbed my greenery!" I said and smiled warmly at her in a peace-love-joy-goodwill-to-all kind of way.

"Oh, I know, honey," she responded with a teeth-whitened-to-blinding-level-brightness smile thrown over her shoulder at me. "You've sure picked out some good stuff here! I am in a *BIG* hurry. You would not believe all I have to get done today! You can get some more for yourself, I'm sure. There's plenty!"

As often happens when confronted with bad manners, I was temporarily flummoxed. I blinked in confusion in an effort to process the hard-to-believe display of bad manners unfolding before my very eyes.

I began a number of responses, none of which actually made it very far:

"Did she just . . ."

"Of all the *nerve* . . ."

"Did that woman just *steal* my greenery?"

"Where was that woman *raised*?"

"Who does that?"

"What is wrong with people these days?"

I was at a loss for words—a rarity for me. I couldn't complete my sentences. That never happens to me. I know some big words, and I use them without apology. Just ask anyone who knows me.

Luckily, I was surrounded by a group of women, none of whom I knew personally, who were riled in my stead in a rather touching demonstration of sisterhood. Yes, indeed, there were witnesses who found plenty of words to describe the Christmas greenery thief. It's quite possible that the woman next to me got a good photo of the naughty one with her cell phone. I hope she posts it on her social media sites. A little public shaming would do that woman a world of good. A viral video post would take her self-important self down a peg or two, and I admit I'd enjoy watching that video myself. I only hoped my slack-jawed visage didn't make an appearance in the post. First of all, I was dressed in flower-arranging attire, so I was comfortable but certainly not stylish. Also, the view of myself in profile horrifies me these days. I just can't believe that's what I look like. I'm glad I only see myself head-on in the mirror. Although that side view looks like me, it can't possibly *be* me . . .

After watching the thief pay for my meticulously selected bits of greenery and seeing her add insult to injury with a final wave to me and a "Thanks again!" tossed in my general direction, it took another two seconds for me to break down into a giggling mess. There was something about the sheer nerve of her move that cracked me up. I had to sit down and gather myself among the poinsettias for a few minutes before beginning my second session of hunting and gathering. People get crazy during the season of peace and goodwill. I never cease to be surprised by that.

ROLL WITH IT

——————————✿——————————

I'VE LEARNED THERE IS no telling what will happen next. It's best to be prepared for anything. Get a flu shot. Learn some Spanish. Fill up the gas tank before you evacuate. Eat the Reese's Cup. Call your mama. Go see the band. Buy the car. Book the dream vacation.

You just never know.

I always have extra contact lenses, a copy of my passport, and my organ donor card with me in my purse. At home, I have a folder clearly labeled "mom's funeral" with explicit instructions for my kids. It's in an accordion folder with my living will, regular will, and a list of passwords to everything in my life.

Even my kids, who can't find a jar of peanut butter in the pantry when it's staring them right in the face and has been sitting on the same shelf for their entire lives, will be able to find my important documents. I've done everything but leave a trail of breadcrumbs or Skittles. I've written a funny list for one of them to read at my funeral. I'm a snob about church music, so no way am I leaving that up to a young priest or a choir that might want to sing some folksy camp song instead of the hymns and anthems I've sung and listened to with joy all my life. Bach is THE MAN, and I love traditional African-American spirituals.

I have set aside money for flowers because I served on the altar guild for many years, and I know what works best in our nave, so there better not be a sprig of baby's breath or a single carnation in sight. I want to make sure there is plenty of food to feed those who show up to grieve my loss on earth. There is nothing tackier than running out of refreshments at a funeral reception. I'll keep an eye on the potential head count as I get older. If I die young, I think I will get a good turnout at my funeral, but if I live to a ripe old age, I doubt many of my friends will be able to attend, so we won't need as many chicken-salad or pimento-cheese party sandwiches from Ousler's. And I want the bar fully stocked—no matter when I go belly-up.

This hyper-planning tendency is not new. I was born this way. On my wedding day, one of my bridesmaids tucked a car key in her bouquet in case I had a last-minute change of heart, and I never leave home without a back-up lipstick. If I get run over by a bus, I want to look my best lying in the road for the young, handsome paramedics who show up to try and revive me.

As you might expect, when I am forced to make big, expensive decisions without time for research, comparison shopping, talking it over with friends, stocking up at the liquor store, or adjusting my attitude, things can get ugly.

Recently, I was tested like Job in the Bible. My house has survived five families before us and nearly 100 years of the vicissitudes of Southern heat and humidity without falling down. This year, all that changed. Like a previously stable country that suddenly falls in an overnight coup, my house fell apart. It was as if the British exchequer suddenly bounced a huge check to pay the grocery bill. We had no hint of impending doom.

Some contagion infected the electrical system and the plumbing with no warning whatsoever. It all started with a leaky faucet in my daughter's bathroom. That faucet was patient zero. Apparently, the illness was airborne. Soon we had an old-house meltdown on our hands. I would not have been surprised to see doctors from the CDC in Atlanta arrive in their scary contamination suits to shut down the whole street.

Like a sweater that unravels when you pull a loose string, my house began to crumble. Literally. The shower leak led to rotten sub-flooring. As each layer of flooring was peeled away, more problems were revealed. Workers had to strip the bathroom tile down to the house's foundation. There were jackhammers IN MY HOUSE! Re-wiring. A dumpster filled with debris. Drop cloths in every room and furniture tented like we'd left it to rot in a Charles Dickens novel.

A new normal emerged from the chaos. My daughter ate sausage biscuits in the kitchen with the workers before she went to school. I ignored the disappointed faces on the days I blew through on my way to work without offering to scramble anyone's eggs.

On the twenty-ninth consecutive day of my life in disarray, I sat with my forehead propped in my hand as I typed listlessly on my laptop and tried to remember why I should care whether the white trim paint I needed to match was "seed pearl" white or "eggshell." Surely that was written down in my house file somewhere, but I could not seem to put my fingers on it.

Our neighbors on one side of our house have a small, yapping puppy that barks nonstop if she is left outside alone. I feel sure she will grow out of it, but that morning, she was feeling particularly abandoned and expressed her dissatisfaction loudly: yap, yap, yap, yap. Yap. Yap. Yap. On the other side of my house, about twelve feet from my kitchen sink, the workers gutting that neighbor's house were listening to their favorite Mariachi band. Again.

I can't write to Mariachi music. I don't have it in me. Lord knows I tried.

That's when the foreman announced the big bad news of the day:

"Mrs. Thompson, I need to show you something."

Translation: "This is going to cost much more than my original estimate."

"And we are out of iced tea," he added, helpfully, on his way back outside to work. This was my cue to brew a fresh pitcher with plenty of sugar to sweeten the work force camped indefinitely in my house like soldiers waiting out a city under siege.

Thousands of dollars we did not have and six weeks down the road, the repairs were completed. There's no new addition. Nothing was remodeled or updated. There is zero visible evidence to justify the large check we wrote. Sure, no one is going to be electrocuted in my daughter's shower—which, apparently, was a horrifying possibility we had no inkling about—and we don't have to flip a breaker every time we turn on the stove and the dishwasher at the same time, but the truth is that we spent a year's college tuition money just to return our house to barely up to code.

Meanwhile, like storm refugees living temporarily in a FEMA trailer, I heated up the grill on the patio to feed my family (stove installation was promised later in the week) and watched as next door a California Closets van pulled in the driveway to customize my neighbor's clothes storage. Sheets of cedar were carefully stacked against the side of the house. I looked on enviously from my patio with my spatula raised as if I were about to conduct a symphony in my bathrobe. The closet designers look askance at the 8 a.m. grilling oddity next door. To me, they seem like rich Parisians looking down from the balconies at peasants below who lack life's most basic amenities—electricity and water. The truth is that nothing, I mean nothing, is more humbling than an inability to flush the potty.

But life goes on. Believe it or not, I taught a class in my house that month, finished several magazine articles, and went about my business the best I could to the background music of power saws and hammering. It could have been worse.

"This is real life," I told my students. "You have to roll with it."

A CANOPY OF STARS

---◆---

I LIKE TINY, LOVELY things: christening gowns, a perfectly iced petit four, dwarf fruit trees, half of an oyster shell, and twinkly strands of fairy lights. As far as presents go, I prefer inexpensive—but obviously well-thought-out—surprises that make me feel special. One of my favorite anniversary gifts was early on when we had zero money for presents. My husband ran a bubble bath for me, lit scented candles all around the bathroom, and placed a gossipy magazine and a chocolate bar on the side of the tub. Then he led me there, shut the door, and said, "I'll watch the kids. Enjoy!" Best. Gift. Ever. These days, I tell my sons one flower says the same thing as a dozen. Be clever. Use your imagination. Only stupid people waste money.

I was reminded of my love affair with small, perfect offerings recently when I attended a destination wedding at a campsite far off the beaten path. The venue was tucked away in a rural county deep in the woods. The wedding reception, dinner, and dancing were set up outside under the stars. And what stars they were! I'd forgotten how different stars look far away from city lights. It was a jaw-dropping sight for a city dweller like me. I might have actually seen a shooting star—*like in a movie.* Really. That's not just the wine talking.

The wedding guests were seated at three long tables, about fifty people each, which were artfully decorated with wildflowers in Mason jars, moss, and simple linens and china. I was happily seated near friends I like to talk to so much that I was comfortable speaking freely—without filtering, worrying, or feeling the need to entertain.

To me, that is a rare gift, one I cherish. It's a liberating experience.

When I leaned back in my seat to take in the whole panorama of the sky above me, it seemed to go on forever. The background was inky blue black with so many stars that those closest to Earth seemed to reflect directly off my dinner plate. I felt like I did when I was a little girl—confident that if I reached up with both of my hands, as far as I could stretch, I could touch a little bit of heaven. The constellations on my right and left seemed to spill onto the far ends of the tables like an optical illusion offered up by my peripheral vision. It was an exquisite, suck-in-a-quick-breath, hold-on-to-your-wineglass moment of wonder for me. I was pleasantly tired, a little tipsy, and glad the sun had gone down, so the heat was bearable, and the stars were a lovely distraction.

It was the same sky I always see, of course. The truth is that if I'd been at home in my usual rut, I likely wouldn't have noticed the stars that night at all. I would have had no reason to look up at the sky. I'd have missed it: a perfect canopy of light. Because I was having so much fun, riding a charming-wedding high, watching an achingly beautiful bride dance with her new husband (and because I allowed myself to enjoy every fattening bite of two pieces of wedding cake—my husband's and my own), my eyes were open—really open—and I was appreciative of the beauty around me.

I want to live more moments like that one.

ICONS

———————✦———————

I LOVE RELIGIOUS ICONS. I'm attracted to them wherever I go in the world, regardless of their specific religious associations. I'm not picky, honestly. Every religion has icons of great beauty. I like the physical representation of saints best; they're my favorites. It's a shame about the endings of those stories, though. Just once I'd like the person I'm rooting for to survive the last chapter. It's very disappointing when the heroes aren't rewarded, and the villains don't get what's coming to them. I appreciate a Disney finale.

I also love paintings, carvings, drawings, and sculptures depicting epic moments in the Bible because they are the stories I grew up with. For me, they are familiar and comforting. I get tactile satisfaction from holding in my hands a tangible reminder of the beliefs I hold dear but often find troubling, distant, and disconnected from my daily life here in the twenty-first century.

I am particularly attracted to icons depicting Mary and her baby. I'm a mother of three children, so I feel connected to her in a personal way. Imagine a woman who had to confess to her family and fiancé that she was pregnant—with the Son of God, no less— even though she was a virgin. That would take hutzpah. I doubt the conversation went well with her parents. Any young woman in her position would have been afraid and worried about being disowned.

I have several iconic versions of the Madonna. My husband says that our children will host a yard sale after we die, and there will be enough icons to satisfy every pilgrim in suburban America. His tone of voice when he says that makes it sound like a bad thing. I don't see why. They're lovely.

Why is the touch and sight of an icon—prayer beads, a stained glass window, a statue, or an illuminated prayer book—so moving to many of us believers? Biblically speaking (and, no, I don't have any qualifications for this type of speculation, but, as you must have realized by now, I rarely let that stop me from thinking aloud), I think it's the same reason Thomas needed to feel where the nails went into Jesus's flesh, the motivation for the women who begged for Jesus's body after his death, and the reason miracles are carefully documented and recounted for succeeding generations. Almost every religion has similar stories of martyrs, heroes, miracles, and exciting historical events, you know. It's not just Christianity.

I find it comforting that although people are killed every day across the globe for their religious beliefs, almost all the theologies ordinary folks like you and I can name actually have a great deal in common. In the end, I think the fate of the world may just depend upon a greater appreciation of our commonality.

In the meantime, icons are a great touchstone for religious followers and nonbelievers, too. Everyone can appreciate the beauty of icons, their historical significance, and their artistic value. We are all part of the human family. We have common ancestors. We use all our senses to experience and learn about the world around us.

It is entirely possible that we are comforted by these physical representations of heavenly things in ways we can't fully understand now. Who knows what will be said about our icons in the centuries to come? I wonder about that sometimes. I'm certainly doing my part to preserve the icon traditions. I feel very virtuous about it.

JOYFUL NOISE

--------◈--------

SINGING IN A CHURCH choir is the most spiritual activity I've ever been involved in. I know that doesn't seem likely if you've never sung in one, but it's true. Singing is about much more than the notes and lyrics on the page. Best of all is the fact that you don't have to be a professional, first-chair singer to reap the rewards of participation. I'm living proof of that.

I look forward to the music on Sunday mornings as much as, and sometimes more than, the sermons. Every sermon isn't preached from a pulpit, you know. In fact, most aren't. These days, the congregation only wants to hear a sermon that lasts about fifteen minutes. That's not much time to address the troubles of the day. One of my favorite quotations, most often attributed to Saint Francis of Assisi, though no one really knows for sure, is "Preach the gospel, and if necessary, use words." That brand of theology rings true for me.

In many ways, the church choir is like a family. There are relatives you like and those you don't. There are troublemakers, peacemakers, hard workers, lazy folks, self-important people, and humble voices. The church is a microcosm of rich and poor and lucky and unlucky. Just like in the larger world, there is every variety of person you can think of in a church: old and young, brilliant, well-educated parishioners and also barely literate and mentally handicapped people. Some individuals are overly generous; others are inexplicably stingy. There are amazingly talented church members and a few who are bitter, beaten down, or mean-spirited. After all, church folk aren't any better or worse than non-church folk.

No matter how big your church is, if you find a small group that is right for you, you will be nourished as an individual, and you will nourish others. I've seen it happen over and over again. I know this advice sounds uncharacteristically evangelical coming from me, an adjective I do not aspire to, so let me clarify: I don't mean simply nourishing people in a religious sense. Churches do more than that.

Societies need a moral center to flourish. That's a well-established premise for many sociologists, anthropologists, psychologists, and historians, men and women who know much more about such matters than I do. Those morals don't have to be my morals, of course. Regardless of one's liturgical beliefs, churches provide comfort, stability, a sense of community, fellowship, food, and social opportunities.

If you are part of a church, you never have to be alone if you don't want to be. Every week, there is something you can do with or for others. The best part: There is no litmus test for members. It's not a country club. Your membership is guaranteed. It does not matter if you are old, sick, poor, unattractive, demented, sad, grieving, addicted, unemployed, or just a generally disagreeable person. The church's mission statement says it has to put up with you. If you're on top of the world, happy at work and home, that works, too. All are welcome.

The world offers no sanctuaries that I can think of on par with the church. Churches have proven their safe-haven value, both literally and figuratively, all over the world and in every conflict in history. Of course, it is also true that more people may have been killed in the name of God than any other cause in history. I didn't say it was a perfect institution.

It took me a while, but I eventually found my church family in the choir section. I've sung in choirs all my life, but I was a member of my church for years before a woman kneeling next to me on a prayer bench one Sunday morning turned to me and declared in a definitive, Mama-knows-best voice:

"You should be singing in the choir."

"I've been thinking about that," I responded.

"How long have you been thinking about it?" she asked.

"About thirteen years," I said.

She snorted, actually snorted at me, grabbed my arm, and frog-marched me up to the choir director.

The director had no idea what kind of puppy was being dumped on her doorstep. Her eyes widened, and she muttered something noncommittal. At the next choir practice, I screwed up my courage and slid into a seat on the back row. (Fair warning: you can't just plop yourself down in a choir chair. Choir folks are weirdly territorial. Seats are often viewed as personal property. I felt like a hot potato for the first few years until I eventually found a spot in the soprano section that didn't ruffle any feathers.) For a few years, I leaned on women much more talented than I am. Now I'm more confident, but I still sing softly. I know exactly what kind of garden-variety soprano voice God gave me.

I've learned more Bible verses by singing them than I ever did by reading them. Although I've read books in every genre you can name (except horror, because I'm not very brave), I was never much of a holy book scholar. Religious fanatics make me nervous. Now, every time I hear scripture readings, sermons, or speeches that reference biblical passages, I hear the verses set to music in my head. For a writer like me, that's handy.

Studying the words, matching them with notes, singing them over and over—repetition required to learn a piece of music well enough to sing it for a congregation—sets them in my long-term memory like nothing else. I think music is deep-seated in our memory banks, and singing is comforting to the mind, heart, and senses. It's soothing to the soul like aloe gel on sunburned skin.

I understand why prisoners sing hymns in their cells. Fannie Lou

Hamer, a woman beaten bloody in the South for her work during the 1960s civil rights movement, sang hymns in her cell. Her body was broken, but her spirit was not. Because I am a Southerner, too, I know that the hymns she sang would have been as familiar to the ears of those who beat her as they were to her. It is impossible for me to understand how anyone could listen to Fannie Lou sing those hymns and remain coldhearted.

When my oldest son began working on a project recording interviews with surviving civil rights workers from previous decades, he called me to ask, "Mom, do you know about Fannie Lou Hamer? Why have I never heard of her? I can't stand what happened to her, Mom. I just can't stand it." He needed me to explain Fannie Lou Hamer. I couldn't do it.

When I sit in my choir seat surrounded by voices—soprano, alto, tenor, bass, and everything in between—I sometimes feel like I'm flying. The voices around me are so rich, colorful, and alive! They jump, skip, soar, fall, cavort, and blend with one another in the sound equivalent of joy, sorrow, or whatever emotion is being conveyed in the musical offering that day. I occasionally close my eyes to savor the sounds that circle like waves around my head, and I have been known to lean back and let the tenors serenade me. They are not always aware that they are singing to me, I admit, but in my imagination, they are. Even church-choir ladies have a fantasy life.

I pray for all the individuals in my choir, the people I've grown to love whose voices make up the joyful noise, and occasionally a discordant few measures—the sounds I associate with God's people on earth muddling through life the best they can, joining forces every week to help each other along the way.

FIREWORKS AND FAIRY LIGHTS

---◈---

WHAT IS IT ABOUT a strand of lights that makes my heart beat faster? I'm a fully-grown woman, and I still smile, gasp, and clap my hands in delight like a kid when I stumble upon an unexpected vista of lights. Holiday lights of any size, shape, or color; long strings of lights above diners in a restaurant; illuminated, big-city storefront windows, neon signs of any type, and tiny fairy lights strewn artfully in a garden—I am entranced by them all. Apparently, a few watts of electricity are all it takes to entertain me. I can't explain why lights evoke this reaction in me. It's a deep-seated response, and I've felt this way all my life.

I am discomfited to admit that I am a female cliché in many ways, but I'm also old enough and self-confident enough that I don't much care what other people think about me anymore. I like what I like, and I love whom I love. One of my favorite pleasures is a long soak in a bubble bath with a trashy novel to read. I believe shoe leather might be edible if deep fried and dipped in chocolate. Children who are singing and signing the lyrics simultaneously make me cry. I would never let a dog or a person go hungry if I could help them, and I value the little things in life most—like lights.

Have you ever driven by a rundown shack deep in the country and been cheered by the sight of Christmas lights tacked optimistically to the crumbling eaves of the house? That's a testament to the power of the human spirit, I think. I believe human beings are optimistic overall, Americans in particular. It's part of our national character. We believe that our individual circumstances can always improve—despite the odds, regardless of our race, gender, sexual orientation, or demographic, and no matter how much overwhelming evidence exists to the contrary. We are sometimes proved right, too.

We love to cheer the underdog; we're proud of our success stories, especially those of immigrants to our nation who have prospered. We love to forgive people, especially politicians and sports figures, and we adore ordinary, against-all-the-odds heroes.

We are a quick-thinking, creative, adaptable people. I think it was a uniquely American spirit that gave the passengers on Flight 93 the ability to absorb the news of the Pentagon and World Trade Center attacks while still in flight and, within about thirty minutes, change the hijacked-airplane mindset of a generation in order to fight back. The rest of the world sometimes sees us as arrogant toddlers, but I love our American spirit, and the rest of the world does, too, when it needs our humanitarian aid, our military prowess, or the largess of our citizens.

Hope. Even to this day, that's what America stands for in the world. That's why so many people want to live here. Even the fireworks on our nation's birthday seem optimistic to me—hope magnified a thousandfold, so powerful and colorful that it explodes in the sky. I like to think of the sparks that cascade down on the heads of ordinary people like you and me as tiny shards of hope.

CRAZY LOVE

"LOVE, SPRING . . . YOU WANT to write about all that?" my editor, Lee Hurley, asked me during one of our hurried cell phone conversations about a magazine freelance piece. Lee speaks quickly in an upbeat, staccato-style shorthand that is always loaded with subtext. I've learned to parse his words carefully. He's my favorite kind of editor: smart and hands-off. I don't like to be bossed around too much. That's because I'm bossy myself, and I always think I know best in any writing situation. I like to think of this as my special gift. God help editors who want to edit my work. They better know what they're doing.

My first reaction to this love-is-in-the-air, welcome-springtime writing prompt was to wrinkle my nose in disdain. I'm sure I threw in a juvenile eye roll, too. I might have made that finger-in-the-back-of-the-throat, I'm-about-to-vomit gesture as well.

I'm not fond of sentimentality. Clichés are the bane of my work as a writing teacher. I have zero respect for writers who lack imagination or originality.

So, how to write about the most clichéd, sentimentalized, overwritten subject in the world? Is there anything left to say that hasn't been addressed in Shakespeare's sonnets? Poems exchanged between Robert and Elizabeth Browning? Movies like *Love Actually*? Stacks of how-to-get-him-or-her-to-love-you books?

Did you know that romance novels are the industry's best-selling books? It's true. And not by a little bit either. I wish I could write them. They're highly formulaic. I like lovers who overcome seemingly insurmountable obstacles and villains who get what they deserve. Everyone should live happily ever after. I'm on board with the genre rules. Bonus for romance writers: Once readers are convinced they can't live without your characters, you can continue a series ad infinitum. If you make it to the top-ten list, the royalty checks roll in like the tide.

Sadly, I don't think I can write romance that will sell. Sometimes I regret being so responsible, safety conscious, well mannered, and just plain ordinary. None of that is going to land me a sexy book contract. I wish I'd written the *Fifty Shades of Grey* trilogy. Although E. L. James isn't going to win a National Book Award, I'm sure she is able to soldier on with the consolation provided by her fat bank account. Now that we all have e-readers, you have no idea what the woman stretched out on the lounger next to you on the beach is really reading. Believe me: it's not *War and Peace.*

The second best-selling genre is mystery novels, which is a natural and predictable progression if you think about it. Boy wants girl. Boy gets girl. Boy later becomes distracted by new girl. Heartbreak ensues. Conflict arises. Everyone loses his or her mind. There is a climactic scene that results in bloodshed, regret, and, upon occasion, Old-Testament-style revenge.

The rise and fall of relationships continue much the same as they always have. Kingdoms are imperiled for love, often of someone ill suited, inappropriate, forbidden, or dangerous—Heloise and Abelard, Romeo and Juliet, and Mark Antony and Cleopatra, for example.

The truth is: I know love exists. It isn't determined by money, good health, physical perfection, gender, or ethnic identification. You can't legislate love. We tried that. It didn't work. You can't reason, beseech, shame, or torture it out of someone. Love even transcends death. Grief is nothing more than frustrated love.

I can't define love categorically, but I know it immediately when I see it, like Justice Stewart's definition of pornography.

The search for love seems to be innate. We don't just want to be loved. We need it. The denial of love embitters us. No matter how old we are, how attractive or unattractive we are, we all seek the in-love high—and to hell with the collateral damage. The French call this buzz *amour fou*: crazy love.

Of course, even something crazy sounds good in French.

THE BUBBLE

———————✦———————

I LIVE IN A suburban bubble. It's safe where I live. I have clean water. The school system is great. More often than not, everyone in the community gets along fairly well. My neighborhood is a mix of old and young, rich and poor, gay and straight, and every ethnicity you can imagine. It's an attractive mix and a wonderful place to live, work, and rear children. And, yes, indeed, I do know how lucky I am.

Most of the time, I don't think about my bubble at all. I'm comfortable here. My friends think the same way I do, mostly. We happily reaffirm our worldviews when we chat on sidewalks outside our homes. I love when people agree with me. Who doesn't? Occasionally, however, my bubble bursts. I'm forced by some troubling event to consider world views radically different from my own. I hate when that happens. It makes me sulky, fidgety, and uncomfortable.

When terrorists strike, either at home or abroad, I can't wrap my mind around it. I can't fathom why someone living thousands of miles away, a man or woman I've never met or exchanged a single word with, hates me, my children, my community, or my country enough to actively seek to kill us. I've never felt that kind of hatred for anyone in the world. My religion is very tolerant of other views. I don't think everyone should adopt my views, and I don't understand why anyone believes that I should adopt theirs or risk persecution or death. Beheading someone in the twenty-first century based on religious, political, or ideological differences leaves me speechless.

I was reminded recently that it's not necessary to travel thousands of miles to encounter narrow-mindedness, bigotry, and prejudice. I didn't enjoy the reminder one bit. I accompanied my husband to a funeral only an hour away from my safe, suburban life. In a small, primitive, rural church deep in the woods, I sat in a crowded, swelteringly hot wooden church pew and listened as a preacher threatened mourners with hellfire, eternal damnation, an end-of-days firestorm, and the wrath of a vengeful God.

I was torn between my inclination to hustle the bereaved family, who I thought deserved better than being yelled at during their loved one's eulogy, out to the parking lot and my desire to rush the pulpit to tackle the zealot spewing venomous, hateful words to the ground and drag him out of the church. I was leaning toward option two, even though I was wearing heels.

I glanced at my husband's face to see if he was on board with either of those plans since he's a lot bigger than I am and would provide excellent backup, and I was shocked to see his face was impassive. He must have sensed I was about to lose all semblance of propriety because he reached out, grabbed my hand, and threaded his fingers through mine without even turning his head to look at me.

"Look at the family," he whispered. "Do they look upset by this?"

I looked. They were all stone faced. They'd obviously heard it all before. This was the funeral they expected. I, on the other hand, was shocked, upset, and offended in about twelve hundred ways.

Nevertheless, I was forced to admit to myself that this wasn't about me. Nobody asked for my approval, permission, or two cents. My job, if I wanted to live up to all my big talk about how I think we should all behave, was to attempt to understand the freaks around me and to find common ground with them. I believe there is always common ground. Sometimes, I admit, it's harder to find than others. I might need Google Earth for this one.

LIFE'S A STAGE

A COUPLE OF YEARS ago I accompanied my daughter to a national high school show-choir competition in Nashville, Tennessee. If you've never been to one of those competitions, you should go at least once for the experience. It's unlike anything else I've ever been a part of. The shows are spectacular. I'm not exaggerating. It's hard to believe that high school directors can get such synchronized choreography, professional dancing, and trained singing from the same children I can't teach to hang up wet towels in the bathroom. It defies logic that the same girls and boys who have split-second timing on stage can't judge the time it takes to drop off their friends and make it home in time for curfew.

The best way to describe this extravaganza is travel-ball dads meet *Toddler-and-Tiara* mamas. Big hair is everywhere. Bling, sequins, and Broadway-style makeup are the order of the day. Backstage is a busy place. Choir director divas and divos scurry in every direction, muttering to themselves about judges, soloists, costume changes, and last-minute substitutions. Set managers hustle to arrange every backdrop you can imagine within a limited time frame, and nervous soloists warm up in dark corners. It's a high-energy day. The audience is friendly, excited to be there, and filled to bursting with former choir members, competing school kids, parents, and fans. Seats are at a premium, and every dash to the bathroom puts you at risk of losing your seat to a more aggressive parent than you are before the next competition starts.

The final round of competition has all the drama of a high school football state-championship game. Even my husband agrees with me on this. (In fact, the whole show-choir experience is very sports-like. I should know. My older children played football, basketball, and baseball. My daughter's choir doesn't call their choir director "Coach" for nothing.)

It was a big deal for high school kids to perform live on the Grand Ole Opry stage, and there were groups from all over the country present to compete. Other national competitions are held across the country in cities like New York, Chicago, and Los Angeles. My daughter's choir regularly attended one or the other, and no, she had no idea how lucky she was.

I sat in my third-row, wooden church pew in the audience, looked up at the miles and miles of red velvet curtain above me, and thought, *I'm sure glad I don't have to write a check for that fabric.* There is no telling how many yards of red velvet fabric it takes to make curtains for the stage at the Grand Ole Opry. It was definitely a special-order situation if I ever saw one.

It was typical of me to worry about the cost of the curtains. Sometimes I think that even if I inherited millions (no threat of that happening in my family), or struck oil in my backyard, I would still worry about money. In my experience, one has to have a whole lot more money than I do in order to be contemptuous about money. I worry about the grocery budget when I order food in a restaurant, which kid has outgrown what when I select clothing items off the sales rack, and if I should really be paying this much to get my hair dyed. Advice: It does not pay to cheap out on hair color. Take my word for it. I've tried it. My bathroom looked like someone had slaughtered a pig in there.

When I was able to drag my brain back to the event at hand, I felt goosebumps pop up on my arms. Seeing my daughter on the stage where so many legends had performed was BIG. I looked at her and thought, *I want to remember this forever.* I doubt my daughter knows the life stories of legends like Hank Williams, Patsy Cline, Minnie Pearl, or Dolly Parton, but I do. If she'd show a bit of interest, I'd share them with her.

This wasn't the first time I felt the weight of all those who have gone before me—saints, sinners, and ordinary people like me. I've felt their presence when kneeling at worn wooden altar rails in churches, while climbing over ancient stone gates and walls, in the dirt under my feet on battlegrounds, and seeping from the walls of prison cells when I've toured historical sites. Blood, sweat, tears, fear, sorrow, joy, hope, dread—strong emotions sometimes seem to become corporeal entities that are absorbed into the inanimate objects around them.

Are you rolling your eyes? Does this kind of speculation make you squirm in your seat? Do you think I have lost my marbles, dropped my basket, or have you experienced this for yourself? It's comforting, in a way, to think that a little bit of ourselves, and the causes we've lived, fought, bled, and sometimes died for, remains behind when we're gone. It serves as an umbilical cord to the future, I think—a tiny smidge of immortality.

THE GROWN-UP CLUB

---◆---

I THOUGHT IT WOULD be a bigger deal. In my mind, I pictured a welcome-to-the-grown-up-club party. I expected flashing lights, clanging bells, and, for some reason, paperwork—something like the documents you need to cross the border from one country to another. I was prepared to pay extra for my mental baggage. I anticipated a few questions from security. In my heart of hearts, I hoped for a shiny club pin, a visible sign of acceptance from the grown-ups in charge that I could attach to my lapel. At the very least, I thought there would be a secret handshake.

In my personal coming-of-age fantasy, I am the star of an after-school-special movie. The lighting is flattering to my face, and the musical soundtrack is both touching and inspirational. As the last scene unfolds, I race down a street lined with senior citizens who smile wisely at each other and nod approvingly at me as I streak by, eager to fulfill my grown-up destiny. In this fantasy film, I am, naturally, firmly toned. Also, I am minus the extra pounds that have dogged me for the last ten years. In the movie's big climax, a much older family member passes the Olympic torch for grown-ups to me. A spontaneous cheer erupts. It's picture perfect.

Of course, this is just a fantasy. That's not how it happened in real life at all. In my experience, real life never works like that. Never. My oh-my-goodness-I'm-a-grown-up-now moment occurred in a dim hallway, deep in a basement riddled with chipmunk-hole faculty offices, on a small liberal arts college campus in Birmingham,

Alabama. At that time, there were ninety-nine faculty members for the entire college. I was the ninety-ninth, the lowliest member, and my basement office was formerly the custodian's broom closet. It still retained the essence of disinfectant in the air.

For an hour, I'd been flipping through handbooks and leaving complicated messages on colleagues' voice mails with a burning question (regarding shifting rhetoric in the English language, in case you're one of the twelve people who actually cares about things like that) that one of my students asked me in the first-ever college writing class I ever taught. I simply did not have a good answer.

This student was learning English as a second language. She was bright and eager. I wanted to help her. I wanted to find the right answer for her. She deserved the truth. (That word should have a warning label attached to it. The word *truth* is a slippery bugger and can get you into a heap of trouble. Trust me on this.) The problem with English grammar, as anyone over the age of ten can tell you, is that many of its rules are idiomatic, which means that there really isn't a good reason for them. They're just the rules. I like to use a sports analogy to explain this. Sports rules are often illogical. People all over the world argue about them all the time. It doesn't matter. It's like when your mother yells, "Do it because I said so!" *Idiomatic* is a fancy way of saying the same thing your mother said when you were a kid.

Exasperated, I stumbled out of my miniscule office into the hall and a bevy of coffee-swigging colleagues. *Perfect timing*, I thought. I couldn't ask for a better group of consultants. I repeated my student's query, word for word, and mentally prepared myself to absorb my colleagues' learned responses like a kitchen sponge so that I could wring out the world's most perfect answer for my student at our next class meeting.

That's when it happened. I had an I-am-a-grown-up-now epiphany. I'm sure you've already guessed it. I'll have you know that those professors didn't know the answer either. The well-seasoned, much-published, long-revered, fully tenured gods of the English department didn't know the answer any better than I did. Even worse, they didn't seem to care one way or another. They weren't the slightest bit embarrassed to be captured in a moment of profound ignorance.

I, on the other hand, was shocked to the core of my being and righteously indignant. "What do you mean you don't know? You have to know!" I argued.

"Why?" the department head asked in a quiet, philosophical, musing tone of voice. He was leaning against my doorframe, peering over my shoulder into my office, showing way more interest in how I managed to squeeze a desk, my computer, and a chair into my office/broom closet than in my professional query.

"What's the big deal?" he asked. "Just explain the rule. The whole subject's in flux. Nobody really knows anymore. Everything changes. Why are you so worked up about it?"

"There has to be someone who knows," I insisted, "somebody to ask."

My colleagues were amused. "There is," they replied. "You. Us. We're the people they ask. Haven't you figured that out yet? We're the grown-ups."

I was horrified. For me, the realization was sharp, shocking, like the time I stuck a Barbie shoe into an electrical outlet. (Oh, who knows why I did it? I was five years old at the time.) I actually sagged against the wall. My mental synapses fired away at a frightening pace, making all sorts of connections. In my imagination, a slideshow of truly alarming images began to loop. I felt the hair stand up on the back of my neck.

When did this happen? When did I become one of the grown-ups, the people who start wars and buy flood insurance and decide what the apostrophe rules are? Young people depend on grown-ups. Old people need them. Grown-ups are the last line of defense. I would have to stock up on bottled water in case of a terrorist attack and remind people to wear sunscreen and change their furnace filters.

I wasn't ready. I wasn't prepared. Sure, I was responsible. I didn't have a criminal record. I paid my taxes, recycled, and showed up for jury duty. Why hadn't I seen this coming? On an admittedly less important although still worrisome point, I am sad to report that for my coming-of-age moment, I was wearing my rattiest sweatshirt and the running shoes I'd been thinking about discarding for the previous decade. If I'd known ahead of time that this was the day for the symbolic changing of the generational guard, I'd have shaved my legs, applied eyeliner, and blow-dried my hair. Well . . . I probably would have. Maybe. If I had time. I definitely would have thought about it. That's the important point.

After about two minutes of total self-absorption, I began to include the rest of humanity in my mental meltdown. I thought of the guy I dated in college who now performs open-heart surgery every day. He's board certified. Nevertheless, in my most vivid memory of him he's hunched over a trashcan throwing up hunch punch after a college mixer. Is it really a good idea for this man to wield a scalpel? I have doubts.

One of the most intellectually challenged humans I ever met in my entire life grew up to be an X-ray technician. Is this a good plan? I worry. Firefighters, dog groomers, stockbrokers, hostage negotiators, parish priests: every person in your high school graduation class grew up to be something. Think about that for a minute. Scary, isn't it? Smart, dumb, kind, or mean as a cottonmouth—the whole colorful kaleidoscope of frail humanity is represented by someone in my address book or yours.

One of my classmates became a senator. No big surprise. Another went to prison. No shock there, either. We're doctors, lawyers, teachers, construction workers, and stay-at-home moms. Every single job a person works matters, and they're all connected to each other and dependent upon one another in a big circle-of-life way. No kidding. This is serious stuff.

In every person's life, there comes a time when all the racing around ends. Someone reaches for you personally, taps you on the shoulder, and says, "Tag! You're it!" Show some gravitas. No need to panic like I did. Nobody is ever really ready. Some of us rise to the occasion. Some of us don't. The one thing you can count on is being "it" at least once in your life—the one who is supposed to know what to do in any emergency. The bad news is that the world is still full of emergencies. The good news is: there's a whole new set of grown-ups every single day. My advice to you is to watch for your moment. It will probably come when you least expect it. It wouldn't hurt to shave your legs, too, just in case.

YUK IT UP

RECENTLY, I CLICKED ON a link to a YouTube video and watched a baby laughing uncontrollably while an adult tore pieces of paper into long strips for the sole purpose of entertaining the infant. Apparently, babies are a friendly audience. They laugh unselfconsciously and loudly at the slightest provocation, and they love repetition. If it's funny once, it's funny the next 100 times, too, in baby world. I would love to get a gig like that. You wouldn't think a comic bit based on tearing paper would work, but it killed.

A top-ten list of what's funny to the under-one crowd reveals paper tearing as the numero uno funniest game in town. Judging by the number of hits on the video, this bit has proved strangely mesmerizing to adults like me, too. I was shocked to see that millions of people had viewed a video that should have been the very definition of boring but, somehow, wasn't.

Nothing about tearing strips of paper seems inherently funny to me. I'm a professional humorist, so I should know. If I've learned anything on the humor speaking circuit, it's that what's funny to one person isn't even remotely amusing to another. This is frustrating and baffling in my line of work. I can read the same essay to different crowds on different nights, and one will laugh so long I have to wait for it to die down before continuing, and the next group will listen to the funny lines without even a hint of a smile. When a previously funny line bombs, I feel like I'm making a joke about Kim Jong-un in front of generals who fear that any giggle that sneaks past their lips will result in a bullet to the head. In North Korea, it just might.

Regardless of one's age or background, a stand-up routine tearing paper seems like a real stretch to me. The definition of funny is one of the most subjective concepts on the planet. Occasionally, I assign a humor essay to my writing classes. They have to define, in a sophisticated discussion, what's funny to them, explain why they find it amusing, research the science behind that, and then analyze and discuss what all that means. It doesn't take long before the class realizes that age, social status, gender, ethnicity, and common experiences all come into play to make a type of humor appealing to one crowd and offensive to another.

There are so many ways to be funny! Some comedy is physical, pratfalls and the like. There is also situational comedy, mistaken identify, confusion and obfuscation, cultural satire, stand-up performances, comedy revolving around props or other add-ons, and more gentle humor outlets like irony, teasing, or gentle satire. Of course, there are as many different reactions to humor as there are types: laughing out loud until you cry or fear you may wet your pants, hoots of laughter, jeering and catcalls, under-the-breath chuckling, soundless grins, wry smiles, even laughter that lights up someone's eyes with obvious humor but doesn't result in a smile at all.

All of those are good reactions for a comedic performer, actor, or writer. Believe me when I tell you that we can feel the response of our audiences, and we feed on that vibe like it's crack. Well, that's how I imagine the high from crack would be. I would never actually do drugs. I'm a control freak, remember? Also, I'm very thrifty. I can't afford the co-pays for the prescriptions covered by my health insurance. Paying for illegal, recreational drugs is beyond my ken.

Almost every type of humor, even the self-deprecating essays I write, offends some reader, somewhere, on some occasion. I think people take themselves too seriously these days and are, overall, as delicate as morning glories come high noon. They need to get over themselves.

One afternoon a woman stood patiently in my signing line with a whole stack of my books. I pegged her for a fan. She made sure to let me know that she was boycotting one of my titles, however, because I made fun of family reunion planners. She thought I'd gone too far with that essay.

"Are you by any chance the family reunion planner in your family?" I asked.

"You betcha!" she answered, all puffed up like a blowfish.

Humor, like beauty, is definitely in the eye of the beholder. Although it's not particularly my cup of tea, Je suis Charlie in every way. Offensive cartoons or animated shows—even extreme social, political, religious, and cultural satires—are not death-penalty offenses. Boycott the publication or streaming app if you want to, sure, but book banning is never, ever the answer.

Some people enjoy crude jokes, crass bathroom humor, or videos of people falling into wedding cakes or being hit in the crotch by baseball bats. That lowbrow, *Three Stooges* humor sets my teeth on edge, makes me tired, and gives me a slight headache, much like the sugar high I get after eating a big piece of birthday cake loaded with frosting. I don't find lowbrow humor any funnier than paper shredding, but clearly I'm not the audience for either one, so it doesn't matter what I think. If the humor lives up to the rule I use for other things—sane, consenting adults—I'm okay with it.

But that baby sure found paper shredding funny. He howled with laughter and eventually keeled over onto his side in pure delight. Imagine laughing so hard you literally cannot remain upright! I'm a little bit jealous. I've certainly never made anyone in my audience laugh so hard he or she fell out of a seat. That would be something, now that I think about it. I would become a legend on the ladies-who-lunch speaking circuit.

Drool spilled out the sides of that baby's mouth and ran down his chin. I've never made anyone do that either. I have been told that some of my readers have done a spit-take when reading something

I wrote. That means they laughed so hard their beverage of choice flew out of their mouths or noses in ill-mannered ways. I consider that quite a compliment.

Like millions of others who watched and listened to the YouTube baby's reaction online, I found myself smiling along with the baby. It wasn't the paper tearing that got to me; it was the baby's reaction. When he began to giggle at the mere anticipation of the next tearing of the paper held aloft by his parent, I laughed out loud right along with him.

Laughter is as infectious as the herpes virus. Why in the world don't we do more of it? Unbridled joy! Why is that such a rare experience for us as adults? We are so stingy with giggles, guffaws, and cackles. What a shame! Laughing is free, good for our souls and bodies, and a cathartic release.

ROCK STARS AND DISHWASHERS

WRITERS MAKE MONEY IN two ways. First of all, we receive royalty checks for the books we write. After a book is finished and edited within an inch of its life, writers send their books out, electronically nowadays, and hope the manuscript finds a good match with a publishing house. The publisher then takes on the risk and expense associated with a book's launch. Yikes!

The other way writers make money is by lecturing on the speaking circuit. Not every writer does this, of course, but I do. There is nothing more fun than autographing a book for a reader. I've had book signings at large festivals where authors are seated, table after table, like Red Cross aid workers handing out relief checks.

Some writers are shy. They barely look up from the books they are personalizing. I think they are missing out on the fun. I enjoy interacting with my readers. You simply would not believe the stories I hear on book tours! I'm telling you—it's one potential Netflix series after another out there. I tell every audience I speak to, "You may be in my next book." I write about my real life, and I don't get out that much.

One of the questions I hear most often is "What is it like to be a writer?" This is usually asked in an awestruck voice as if writers were rock stars. Occasionally, I do feel like a rock star. I love my reader groupies. Who wouldn't? I'd be lying if I didn't admit that it's wonderful to be picked up from the airport, dropped off at a swanky hotel, and wined and dined by interesting people, usually readers, I'd never have otherwise met. On rare occasions, while waiting in a green room for a television interview, I get to mix and mingle with real stars, political figures, and people in the news. That's fascinating—like meeting the real-life characters from a book or movie.

Speaking comes easily to me. It doesn't feel like work at all. It feels like a visit with friends. I can always gauge the mood of an audience I'm entertaining. When they laugh, I feel powerful. My goal is to entertain. Everyone has problems. I'm paid to be a fun distraction. I can tell when my audience is riveted by words I've written just for them; it's a two-drink high. Nothing beats that feeling.

I always talk, read a bit, and then open myself up to questions. I'm not a politician; I'm very humble, and I have nothing to hide. It's my favorite part of the day because I never know what I will be asked. Sure, some questions come up again and again: "How did you get your first book published?" "Where do you get your ideas?" and "What do you like to read?" But there is always a random question that comes from who knows where that makes me laugh. I then get to use that question to play with the audience a bit. For example, I've been asked, "Where did you get that dress?" "Do you think of yourself as a 'real' writer?" and "Can I take you out to dinner after this?"

On the other side of the coin, sometimes I'm not queen for the day at an event—not at all. I'm the hired help, one rung below the dishwasher. I've been the headliner for events where no one greeted me, had a signing table ready, or thought about the logistics of microphones, book sales, etc. I've spoken to groups that did not offer me so much as a glass of water or access to a restroom. I've spent hours traveling to a venue only to find that no effort has been made to publicize the event, as if I should be able to magically conjure up an audience in the wake of my car.

I've been banished to the dark corners of bookstores, ignored by their proprietors, or paraded about for hours before an event like a circus oddity. Sometimes, book fans talk about me to one another as if I am not present and obviously able hear them. I try not to take these slights personally. It's all part of the job, and the good parts of the job far outweigh the bad parts.

Everyone has a day job, you know. Writing just happens to be mine. I bet my job isn't that different from your job. Even the most glamorous-seeming jobs have a not-so-shiny side, too. It's good to remember that. My job requires me to make people I've never met in my life laugh out loud, which isn't always easy to do. But when I succeed, I know I've done a good day's work. It takes me hours to come down from that.

TEACHERS LIKE ME

TEACHERS LIKE ME BELIEVE that if we can make a difference in just one student's life, we can change the world. Typically, teachers are realistic, practical people. We have to be. We know we won't be able to help every student, no matter how hard we try or wish we could, but we can live with that reality because we know that we will make a difference for at least one. I'll be the first to admit that this is a bold philosophy.

Every experienced teacher can tell you a story like the one I'm about to relate. Ask around. Even as I type, I know it may sound hokey to some of you, but I believe the make-a-difference theory with all my heart. If I didn't, I wouldn't continue to teach.

I love teaching college students more than any job I've ever had in my life. I knew early on that I would be sued, shot, fired, or arrested if I taught young kids. I would probably deserve it, too. I don't have the patience for that work. I expect kids to behave. I made my own kids behave. If the children I was teaching failed to conform to my expectations, there would be consequences. I do not bluff. You can ask my kids about that. I'm well matched with young adults.

In particular, I like to teach smart students. Some people have a gift for struggling students or special-needs kids, but that's not for me. I know my gifts. I like to take bright students to the very brink of their potential and then shove them right over the edge. I even enjoy their screams on the way down. I know they'll land on their feet because I teach them what they need to know to be successful in my class and others.

Over the years, I've gotten good results with my approach. I'm proud to say that I still hear from former students occasionally, and there is one Christmas card I get every year from a former student that makes me feel like a superhero. The card arrives with no fanfare and only a signature, but it reassures me that a young man who appeared in my office one day to tell me he was fed up with his basketball coach and dropping out of college is doing okay.

From the moment he appeared in my office doorway all those years ago, his dramatic announcement did not go the way he'd planned. First of all, I simply refused to accept his decision to drop out. He obviously did not see that coming. I dragged him into my office, pushed him into a chair, sat in the one right beside him, got in his face, and started arguing. I'm good at it. I used every debate-team trick in the book. I pleaded my case like he was the Unites States Supreme Court, and I'd been polishing my brief for the last decade.

I also used a secret weapon: guilt. I know using guilt to ensure compliance is frowned on these days, but I didn't care. I pulled out every arrow in my quiver and shot them as fast as my fingers could pull back the bow. Fear and guilt have been useful parenting tools for generations of moms. That's because they work. I used the sticks and carrots available to me at the time. I make no apologies for that.

Parenting—like teaching—is often akin to the clichés about sausage making and passing a bill through Congress. It's not always pretty. In my roles as parent and teacher, I'm interested in results. I did not have time to quibble about the process when my student was about to throw away a basketball scholarship.

I also made him feel guilty for letting his family down. I didn't pull any punches, and I felt not one shred of remorse about that. I tell my own kids all the time: "I don't care what you think about my decision right now. When you're forty, if you still think I was wrong, we can talk about it then."

I showed my student scary dropout statistics online. I threatened to call his mama and tattle on him. I was dogged about talking him out of quitting. When he refused to listen to me anymore and stormed out of my office, I ran along beside him on the sidewalk to keep up (no easy feat—I'm 5'2", and college basketball players are tall) and argued fiercely with every stride.

When he slammed his car door in my face, you'd think I would have gotten the message. There was nothing subtle about it. But I was a teacher on a mission to save a good kid from himself. I followed him to the airport, parked in short-term parking, found him seated in a restricted area, and, when I could get no closer without a ticket, I leaned over the rail, turned up the volume, and took up the fight right where I left off.

Eventually, as I'm sure you've guessed by now, I convinced him to stay. It's possible he gave in just to shut me up. I can live with that. It worked. No college kid wants a professor to become a stalker. I was definitely headed down that road. When he finally caved, he followed me from the airport to my house. He ate macaroni and cheese with my children and gave my son tips on his three-point shot on the basketball goal in our backyard. For me, that day is forever engraved in the win column.

I'm proud to report that my student graduated from college and graduate school and works as an accountant today. He supports a family, and he claims that the main reason he didn't drop out back then was because he couldn't bear to disappoint me. He knew I wouldn't give up.

That story is my proudest teaching moment. Each of us is a teacher or mentor to someone in our lives—whether we realize it or not. Look around you. You might be surprised by who looks up to you.

BELLE LETTRES

I WISH I HAD attractive handwriting. Imagine a grocery list jotted down in Spencerian script, as opposed to my usual illegible scrawl. Items like "drain cleaner," "kitty litter," and "ground chuck" would look positively poetic in that hand. With practice, my handwriting could become a thing of beauty in itself—elevating the ordinary and humdrum to something grand.

I sang in a choir once with a young woman who taught herself calligraphy so that she could address her own wedding invitations. Thrifty and pretty—how delightful! When I received my invitation in the mail, I took the time to really study it because I know the work that went into it. The gold ink was unusual. Each word was big and bold, and the hand-lettered names and addresses took up almost the entire envelope. I felt like Cinderella opening an invitation to the royal ball. I love attention to detail—in all things.

Almost no one handwrites letters anymore. The daily arrival of the post used to be a touchstone in the day for many people. These days my husband and I check our mailbox every few days instead of every day. Not much of importance comes to us through the mail. Along the same lines, although we still pay for a landline to our home (mostly because it's impossible to figure out how to "unbundle" it from the rest of our gadgets), we rarely answer it. It's always sales calls. People who know us call our cell phones. Snail mail and shared house phones are relics of the past.

When I receive a newsy letter from friends or relatives, as opposed to the usual bills, ads, and political flyers that crowd my mailbox, it's like discovering a tiny present. It's thrilling! I savor opening the letter, read it through several times, and feel grateful that someone took the time to write to me in such a personal way. I have letters so beautifully written that I could not bear to throw them out squirreled away in between the pages of books all over my house.

I peruse letters I receive today with an accompanying cocktail in a tranquil spot, as if I'm an actor in a coffee commercial. That's because the receipt of a letter feels like an event of import, not something to be opened in the car while waiting for the light to change—something more like the formal reading of a will and testament where personal farewell letters, which have been left in the care of a solicitor, are distributed to friends and family in a made-for-television moment.

The content of such letters seems potentially dramatic, an unveiling machination to further the plot in a BBC series. Perhaps someone I love has a secret lover, a previously undisclosed illness, or a stash of drug money hidden in a spot only I can retrieve in time to pay the ransom and free my cousin. Sure, all that's unlikely, but a girl can dream. Any one of those scenarios would be preferable to opening the sewer bill or a coupon for half off our next food delivery.

Nowadays, like everyone else, I get emails and texts. I rarely even talk on the phone anymore. It's not the same! I feel a loss with the one-way communication we favor now. I think we've taken a giant step backwards in how we relate to one another. To be satisfying and nourishing, communication requires simultaneous, two-way interaction, at the very least. Have we all forgotten the most basic requirements for social engagement?

I fear we've lost something important by abandoning handwritten correspondence. Throughout history, letters have served as remarkable records of the world's big-screen happenings. They flesh out the dry statistics of historical facts with local color, personality, and commentary. Belle lettres give a voice to ordinary citizens, particularly women and oppressed, powerless members of societies all over the world, those who are often deemed too unimportant to have their lives immortalized by traditional record keeping.

I treasure the letters I find tucked away from family members who died long before I was born. The pages of their letters to friends and family make them come alive for me. We are all more than the birth and death dates we leave behind in graveyards and courthouses. Even the most boring person is more interesting than that.

When I teach writing, I always devote one class to letter writing. That's how important I think it is. I urge you to write a letter today to someone who means something to you—a relative, friend, former teacher, or coach. Send them notes of thanksgiving, praise, or love. At the very least, share a juicy morsel of gossip, make an outrageous prediction, or offer an amusing observation. I bet you'll be surprised by the response you get. I promise it will be worth it.

WHOOPSIES

———————————◆———————————

PEOPLE SAY STUPID THINGS. Sometimes they don't know what to say, but they feel a pressing need to say something, so they say the wrong thing, assuming that saying anything is better than saying nothing. Sadly, this is rarely true.

At funerals, for example, well-intentioned mourners often struggle to come up with the "right" words to comfort the bereaved. What comes out is often awkward, callous, and, upon occasion, cringe-worthy.

I've heard comments about how good the deceased looks in his coffin. I bet you have, too. Does anyone believe this is really something a teary widow wants to hear? In what way is this observation helpful? And how in the world should the polite widow respond?

"Well, yes, Aunt Virginia, considering he's dead, I think he looks pretty good, too" perhaps? Let me clear this up: If you can't think of something comforting to say when someone dies, the words "I'm sorry" will suffice. They're hard to beat. Classic. Traditional. Short. Unlikely to result in unintended linguistic consequences.

We've all been guilty of tossing off a glib comment, words we immediately wish, two seconds after they pass our lips, we could cram back down our throats to be swallowed whole and never heard from again—like a pelican determinedly swallowing a whole, freshly scooped fish. The words we hear in our head often sound different when they ricochet like machine-gun fire around a room. Once those words are fired, it's too late to do anything except absorb the resulting flak the best you can. Collateral damage is inevitable.

In a white-hot flash of temper—or when our partners, children, politics, or jobs make us nuts—that's when we are in danger of allowing our mouths to spout off a stream of words without a thoughtful preview from our brains. Most verbal gaffs are simply the result of a failure to filter.

In diplomatic circles, such mistakes are called whoopsies. Don't you love the onomatopoeia? I do. I get an instant mental picture of "whoopsie" when I say the word out loud, like someone is waving a flash card with the word in bold, black font.

Those of us who overhear such statements wince in sympathy and thank our lucky stars that we didn't say something worse ourselves. Heaven help you if you're a public figure with foot-in-mouth disease. The media will play your linguistic faux pas on a twenty-four-hour loop until someone more famous than you makes an even bigger whoopsie.

We all know a few people who purposefully toss verbal hand grenades into the conversation, simply because they love to incite chaos among colleagues, friends, and volatile family members. I'm sorry to say that the world has some mean folks walking around with the verbal equivalent of IEDs always at the ready to spice up the Scrabble board of life. I bet you already knew that.

When you hear one of those grenades clatter at your feet, you could scramble around on your hands and knees and try to cram the pin back in, but that only works in old, black-and-white war movies. Option two: roll your eyes and tighten your lips in disapproval. Rally your indignation. Demand a retraction on the spot if it makes you feel better.

Then . . . let it go, like you're Queen Elsa in *Frozen*.

An apology is the only redress available, and if someone is too ornery to cough one up, remember these words: you can't fix stupid. That's the genetic lottery at play in the world. Ignorance can be overcome, but stupid is forever. Stupid people say stupid things. That shouldn't surprise anyone.

Resist the temptation to smack stupid people on the head with a garden gnome. It might be gratifying for a moment or two, but it won't do one thing to change the mind of the stupid person. Also, it's a felony to assault someone with a garden gnome. Stupidity is not a crime. Yet. Anyway, it's not your job to go around smiting stupid people. It's best not to resort to violence. Genetic weeding takes a few millennia. You must be patient like you are waiting on the stalactites and stalagmites to meet in the middle of a cave.

I admit: it's hard to be tolerant, especially when someone makes a spectacularly stupid statement like "The Holocaust never happened" or "9/11 was an American conspiracy."

I don't know where people come up with this stuff. Some people should not have Internet access, that's for sure. Here's my advice: avoid the crackpots whenever possible—even if they're family. Educate the ignorant when you can, but be nice to stupid people. They really can't help themselves.

ONE SURVIVOR'S STORY

I ONCE WALKED A few blocks down the street to a branch of the public library tucked conveniently in my neighborhood to hear a Holocaust survivor speak about his experiences during WWII. Every day, it seems, the last few handfuls of these firsthand witnesses to one of the most horrific chapters in human history are silenced by death, age, and infirmity, so I felt a sense of urgency to attend that night.

I've been interested in Holocaust literature as long as I can remember. For a year, when I was about twelve, I read everything on the Holocaust I could get my hands on, which wasn't much in a small town before the Internet. The first book I remember reading after *The Diary of Anne Frank*, every middle-schooler's entree into the genre, was Corrie ten Boom's *The Hiding Place*. I thought it was a real spy thriller; there were even messages hidden under upside-down postage stamps! I turned every page hoping that the sisters would survive their concentration camp internment, and I rejoiced alone in my bedroom when fleas kept one of the most feared guards away from them. The Jews the ten Booms risked their lives to hide seemed as real to me as neighbors on my own street.

The reading I steeped myself in all those years ago stood me in good stead all my life. I feel sorry for people who didn't have the opportunity to read in childhood or didn't enjoy reading until adulthood. They never really catch up. There is nothing like the feeling I had back then when there was always a stack of books waiting for me by my bed, and time didn't seem to flow along in analog fashion like it does now. I felt like I had all the time in the world to read whatever struck my fancy. I could spend an entire afternoon in a hammock in the backyard meandering through Middle Earth, Narnia, re-reading *Little Women,* or indulging my reading fantasies with formulaic romance novels. In short, I had time to read and a library card. That's the best gift a child could ever receive.

One of my fondest memories of my mother is trailing in her wake as she marched into our small-town library to inform the librarian, who was a bit of a martinet, that I was free to read *any* book in the library—not just the ones deemed age-appropriate for me by the librarian on clearly marked, grade-by-grade shelves. I am grateful to this day that I had a mom who read, encouraged me to read, and had zero tolerance for censorship. We were frequent fliers at the library. I was reminded of my mom's example when my own children were young, and I had to stand up to a friend who was vocal in her objection to the Harry Potter series. She called it "trash." I read the first one that she dropped off at my door in one night and found it charming, wonderful, and beautifully written.

I'm glad to have come of age when children were still allowed to entertain themselves. I didn't need a color-coded activities calendar. It was socially acceptable to be unscheduled and a little bored. My afternoons and evenings were not overburdened with sports practices, club meetings, school and volunteer activities like my own children experienced until we all fell into bed at night with exhaustion.

I took for granted the luxury of huge chunks of non-earmarked time when I had it. I know reading Holocaust literature is not everyone's dream for their precocious child reader, but I think it's entertaining to stumble across children with a passion for dinosaurs, royal family histories, ship-building, or any other subject about which the breadth and depth of their knowledge rivals that of any adult—simply because they have the time to read for hours and hours without guilt or interruption.

Nonfiction storytelling, eyewitness accounts, like the one I was about to hear, is like listening to books come alive. I am thrilled to hear personal stories, especially those with ties to significant historical events like WWII, 9/11, or the civil rights era.

This survivor's story was different than any I had heard before. From the age of six until he was nine and a half, he was hidden from the Germans by various families in Holland. His family split up, hid in separate locations, and survived the war, but not without terrible scars, of course. They were eventually reunited, but the deep familial connections to one another were lost. This survivor came to love the family that took him in as his "real" parents. The bond remained strong for the rest of their lives.

I was surprised when this survivor told the audience that this was the first time he had ever spoken publicly about his experiences during the war. Even though he participated in the Steven Spielberg archive project and sent the files to his children, he still didn't discuss his experiences with them one-on-one. That seems particularly telling to me. He and his sister, although close, never spoke of their years apart. That silence speaks of trauma, I think.

There were another ten or so Holocaust survivors in the audience, and they were asked to stand and be recognized. It was an emotional moment for everyone in the room. I wondered if they knew the speaker personally or if they had merely heard of the local event and wanted to show their support like I did. There is nothing in the world that can take the place of a primary account of suffering. I felt the weight of his "first telling" as I stood against the wall listening to his story in the overheated auditorium of the library.

I believe that all of us in the audience—indeed, all who hear the tale—take on a duty to bear witness. I was proud I'd brought my son with me to hear, firsthand, of these atrocities, especially in the twenty-first century when many people discount the stories of Holocaust survivors, in particular the fringe media outlets. This man's story was one of deep loss, triumph, survivor's guilt, and moments of irony and happenstance.

If it had not been for the teenage girl who opened her window to warn him that her father was going to turn him in, he would have been rounded up by the Germans and murdered. He has no idea why she showed him that kindness. After his first marriage failed, broken beyond repair by his wife's experiences in Bergen-Belsen, this survivor eventually married again—to a German, non-Jewish woman. I'm amazed by that even as I write about it years later. I'm not sure I'm open minded and forgiving enough to have gotten to that point in the years right after the war—if ever.

Over and over he spoke with gratitude about the citizens who risked their own lives to save him and his family. At the same time, he acknowledged that the Holocaust could not have happened without the wholesale betrayal and complicity of thousands of other ordinary citizens who did nothing. That is a painful truth. To this day, it is hard to hear. He said his father always reminded the family, "You can't judge them for betraying us. If the situation had been reversed, what would we have done?"

I don't think any of us could say with absolute certainty what we would have done. Oh, we can say what we hope we would have done, or what we think we should have done, but that's not the same thing at all. It's hard to be that honest with ourselves. If the lives of my own children were at stake, what wouldn't I do? Not much. Would I betray my country? My faith? Would I sacrifice another mother's child to ensure the safety of my own? I'm not sure.

The world is still dangerous and uncertain. The specifics may change over the years—different enemies, borders, and threats—but the question of what each of us is willing or unwilling to risk for the sake of others is still relevant today. Evil exists. We all come face-to-face with it and have to make choices, large and small.

For me, Elie Wiesel says it best: "The opposite of love is not hate, it's indifference. The opposite of beauty is not ugliness, it's indifference. The opposite of faith is not heresy, it's indifference. And the opposite of life is not death, it's indifference between life and death."

MY DAY AT
THE MUSEUM

---❦---

ALABAMA JUST OPENED A new world-class museum in its capital city of Montgomery—the Legacy Museum. The outside part (a few blocks away), the National Memorial for Peace and Justice, has been awarded a National Park landmark designation. That's not small potatoes! For the first few weeks, it was too crowded for my family to get tickets online, but after about a month, we were able to secure our time slots to tour, and we lined up outside the front doors with a film crew from California, tourists from New York, and a horde of children on a field trip. It was a scorching day, and we were all anxious to get inside the air-conditioned venue. The sun beat down on us mercilessly, and most of the conversations revolved around the heat, a subject easily navigable for visitors of all ages, races, and backgrounds.

There is nothing easy about visiting a museum dedicated to the history of lynching in America. Not one thing. I thought I was ready, but I wasn't. Not really. How could any self-aware, well-educated, feeling human being be ready for that? It wasn't a summer outing I embarked on for fun. Much like touring a concentration camp site in Germany, a prisoner-of-war memorial in Hanoi, or anywhere in the world where there are markers to note human cruelty or horror imposed on a powerless group of people by a powerful one, I went because I owe it to those who died to remember, to bear witness, to acknowledge the legacy of suffering, and to teach my children our collective history so that we prevent such things from happening in the future. It's that simple. Sometimes, the job of being human is just to show up.

Attorney Bryan Stevenson is one of Alabama's treasures. His work at the Equal Justice Initiative is one of the driving forces that made the museum possible. His cause: mass incarceration reform. Thanks to his work and that of many others, a museum now stands on the site where slaves were warehoused not that many years ago. It will educate visitors about the more than 4,400 verified, recorded, undeniable-to-anyone lynchings that took place in over 800 counties all over the country—in all the states you'd expect and many that might surprise you.

As I looked at the dirt from lynching sites displayed in clear glass jars, I was reminded of the commendation prayer for the dead in the *Book of Common Prayer*: ". . . we are mortal, formed of the earth, and to earth shall we return." I harkened back to a lifetime of Ash Wednesday services, and I could almost feel the pressure of my priest's thumb on my forehead as he made the sign of the cross with Lenten ashes collected from the burning of last year's Easter palms while I knelt at the altar rail and contemplated my long laundry list of transgressions. The jars of dirt, all a little different in texture and hue, seemed important to me. Each marks the snuffing out of an individual life in the world—like the fistfuls of soil that dribble through the fingers of family members over a coffin at a graveside service.

As a white woman, I had the same fear when I toured the Legacy Museum that I had the first time I toured the Civil Rights Museum in Birmingham, AL, where I live: I was afraid I'd see the face of someone I love in the photographs on the walls—either as a victim of racism, segregation, or injustice or as the perpetrator, co-conspirator, or the silent enabler or bystander. There are sins of omission and commission that stretch out, both for individuals and for nation-states, and bleed across generations. Nobody knows that better than Southerners.

The Legacy Museum handles its subject matter carefully, sensitively, and with dignity. That's not easy to do with a subject as visceral and intrinsically obscene as lynching. There is a natural progression as you tour the museum, and you can go through at your own pace, reading as much or as little as you'd like along the way. The photographs are chosen carefully for effect, but it's not a bombardment of shock waves or sensory overload. The museum visitor doesn't feel under attack, regardless of skin color, and the information is meticulously researched, professionally presented, and informative—a world-class endeavor. I'm sad beyond words that this museum exists in the world, but I'm as proud as I've ever been of my state that it came to fruition here, right here in the capital of the Confederacy, where ugliness lived and breathed in the hot, humid heart of slavery and segregation.

I expected to be overwhelmed with emotion during my first visit to this museum. It's a lot to take in. But I was surprised by what took me to my knees: it was the mothers. The mothers in photographs seemed to stare right at me, personally, across the years. In handwritten letters on the back wall, mothers pleaded for mercy for themselves and their children. It reminded me of nights when I've walked the floors of my own home worrying about the children I gave birth to. While the children in the museum photographs are not my children, they are somebody's children.

The angry eyes and resolute shoulders of women photographed at church services and political meetings spoke to me in a language I understood. I grew up attending church meetings, too. As a lifelong choir member, I know every note of the music playing softly in the background of interactive exhibits and sung by mothers raising their hands to heaven from church pews—the deep altos, the syrupy mezzos, and the high-soaring sopranos dancing their way up and down the stave in the complicated harmonies of the hymns, anthems, and spirituals we now associate with human rights struggles around the world. Most importantly, everywhere I turned in the museum, I came face-to-face with mothers like me, black and white, who were fellow visitors on the day I toured.

When I started blinking back tears, a young black man, in his early twenties, I'd say, pulled a tissue from the plastic packet tucked in the front pocket of his pants and handed it to me. He was an intern, I think, trained by the museum to respond to the distress of visitors like me.

"You are not old enough to completely get this," I told him. "I remember more than you, and I wasn't even alive for most of it. It's the mothers. I can't bear to see the mothers," I struggled to explain. "I'm a mother, too."

"Yes, ma'am, I understand," he responded, kindly—not because I'm a mother, or white, or older, not so much a gesture of respect as a knee-jerk response from a young man reared in the South. "Yes, ma'am" is a social custom where we live, the way sweet children are taught to address their beloved mothers. The irony of him comforting me was not lost on either of us. The South is complicated like that.

I hope you will visit the Legacy Museum and bring your extended family with you. I want everyone to visit—ordinary men, women, and children—not just Hollywood filmmakers, graduate students, high school kids on school-mandated field trips, and those who are passionate about social justice causes. If ordinary people who live ten minutes, two hours, or one state away fail to show up, if they ignore this museum's existence because it's an uncomfortable reminder of history, then we will have compounded the sins of our ancestors and made a clear statement to our children and grandchildren about its importance. The mission of the museum will remain unfulfilled; its influence will be diluted, and we will have made yet another one-step-forward-and-two-steps-back mark on our historical timeline of progress. But if this museum stays crowded, and history professors stand next to middle school students, and stay-at-home moms tour shoulder to shoulder with prominent political activists and elected officials, then my home state will have done something memorable, unique, just, and . . . kind.

ACKNOWLEDGMENTS

THERE WERE MANY TIMES when I was writing this book, my fifth, that I wondered if it would ever make it to the shelves. My beloved publisher changed hands suddenly, and the publishing world is hard to decode these days. Since publishing my last book, I went back to teaching full time on a small college campus and accepted umpteen freelance magazine assignments. This manuscript took a backseat to almost everything else. I returned to it every few months to make some desultory revisions, and then I forgot about it again for a long time. Some days I was happy with it. Other days, I wanted to trash the whole thing.

This book is different from my earlier books. It's still creative nonfiction, my genre of choice, but it's not all laugh-out-loud funny. It has some heft to it. I wasn't sure if my readers would welcome this new phase or if they'd reject it out of hand.

Change is inevitable, you know. Writers like me change and grow. What matters to me, what tugs at my heart, and the random events of the world that inject themselves into my tiny life beg to be written about differently over time. Trying to write the same way, to follow a previously successful pattern, that's stifling—even though it would be financially rewarding. My husband wants to cry a little about this.

The one constant in my writing life: the people who love and support me. Without them, I would never be able to find the words.

To my dear ones, as always, thank you. I couldn't face the day without you in my life. If I had to name one great blessing in my life, it would be that I have always had good friends. Most of all, this time, thanks to Whitney, Phyllis, Vivian, Tricia, Gonzo, Andrea, Vera, Beth, Angie, Brit Huckabay, friend and photographer, and my St. Stephen's parish folk.

To the colleagues and work friends who share my days on the Hilltop, thank you for listening to me rant and supporting me. Most especially, thanks to Dave Ullrich (who needs to get his own book out, and I've given him a deadline, by God), Jody Stitt, Will Hustwit, and Tynes Cowan, talented writers themselves, and my champions all. To you, I offer my humble, heartfelt thanks for listening. More thanks to the home team, especially Sandra, Michael, Jane, Kim, Barbara, and Debbie.

Thanks to Jake Reiss at the Alabama Booksmith in Birmingham, AL. He believed in this book—and in me—even when I had doubts. Without his encouragement, you wouldn't be reading this book. Thanks to SIBA, especially, and independent booksellers all over the country who read, know their authors, and hand-sell our books. Stay strong!

Thanks, too, to my Birmingham-Southern College students, past and present. Nothing makes you a better writer yourself than teaching other people to write every day. To teach, you really have to know your stuff. MRT loves you!

Thanks to family, too: parents, sister, cousins, aunts, and, most especially, the ungrateful wretches, Warner (the only person I asked to read the manuscript before publication—thank you, baby boy), Nat, and Lily.

Finally, as always, thanks to my husband, Bill, who is frequently introduced at public events—I'm not making this up—this way: "You all know our sweet Judge Thompson . . . and his wife." I just know his campaign staff holds their collective breath every time I'm handed a microphone.

Most of all, thanks to those of you who read and buy books. Without you, I wouldn't have the best job in the world.

CPSIA information can be obtained
at www.ICGtesting.com
Printed in the USA
BVHW082116170220
572579BV00012B/1350

9 781633 939974